OFFICIAL'S MANUAL:
TOUCH AND FLAG FOOTBALL

OFFICIAL'S MANUALS

from Leisure Press

TOUCH AND FLAG FOOTBALL

John W. Reznik
And Rod Grambeau
University of Michigan

1979/88 pp./paper $2.25
ISBN 0-918438-46-2

> **OFFICIAL'S MANUALS**
>
> only **$1.35 each** on **1-time purchase of 10 or more copies (any combination)**

BASKETBALL

Gary Miller
Cal State - Northridge

1979/72 pp./paper $2.25
ISNB 0-918438-47-0

VOLLEYBALL

James A. Peterson
And Lawrence S. Preo

1979/96 pp./paper $2.25
ISBN 0-918438-48-9

SOFTBALL

Robert Clickener
University of Illinois

1979/72 pp./paper $2.25
ISBN 0-918438-49-7

SOCCER

Nick Kovalakides
University of Maryland

1979/100 pp./paper $2.25
ISBN 0-918438-50-0

> • Use as a reference • Issue to your sports officials • A valuable aid for programs at *all* levels

OFFICIAL'S MANUAL:
TOUCH AND FLAG FOOTBALL

John W. Reznik, Ph.D.
and
Rodney J. Grambeau, Ed.D

Leisure Press
P.O. Box 3
West Point, N.Y. 10996

A publication of Leisure Press.
P.O. Box 3, West Point, N.Y. 100996
Copyright © 1978 Leisure Press
All rights reserved. Printed in the U.S.A.

ISBN 0-918438-46-2

Credit for cover photographs:
Upper left - James A. Peterson
Upper right - Jeffrey Carr
Lower left - James A. Peterson
Lower right - Kathy Koch

Illustrations by:
Gini Pearson

CONTENTS

Chapter

5

CHAPTER I

The Game

The origin of touch and flag football is an integral part of the saga of the overall development of "football." Unfortunately, the exact date and circumstances of the evolution of touch and flag football are unknown.

A species of touch football called "camp ball" was played by both sides in the War Between the States. There is also some evidence that a form of touch football was played by United States troops during the periods of the Spanish American War and World War I. Also prior to World War I, an early type of touch football was played by grade school- and high school-age boys in New Orleans.

The United States armed forces developed and popularized touch football during World War II. Through their efforts, it became, perhaps, the major mass participation game in the United States. It is interesting to note that this military version of touch football was almost always played with eleven players on a side. During World War II, several million soldiers played touch and flag football. Their uniforms consisted of a variety of clothing, from OD woolens to blue denims, sweaters, undershirts and shorts. Competition was conducted from Alaska to Australia, from Ireland to Iceland, from India to China the year around.

After World War II, both GI's and physical training personnel introduced touch and flag football to college campuses, to school recreational grounds, to play areas and parks in cities and towns and to the recreation yards of industrial plants. Even today, the armed services are still among the strongest supporters (participation-wise) of both touch and flag football.

The popularity of touch and flag football has continued to grow unabated since World War II. Men and women of *all* ages are participating in organized leagues at all educational levels—elementary, junior high, secondary, and college. Community-run programs are also highly popular. In addition, in recent years, a new form of touch and flag football has been added to many programs—co-recreational leagues. Teams composed of an equal number of men and women compete against each other. A limited number of modifications in the rules are made to account for physiological differences between men and women.

The rigorous nature of the game, coupled with the fact that it can be played by men and women of all ages and skill levels, ensures that touch and flag football will remain as one of the most popular team-participation sports in the United States.

CHAPTER II

Do's and Don'ts for Good Officiating

Although for most individuals officiating touch and flag football games is only a part-time job, in order for it to be an enjoyable and rewarding experience, adhering to specific precepts is both necessary and helpful. An uncompromising adherence to these precepts will enable officials to be better prepared to fulfill their responsibilities and duties in an effective manner. These precepts—listed as do's and don'ts—apply to officials at all levels of competition.

Do's

1. Acquire a knowledge of the rules and their proper and correct interpretation and application. This will allow the game to progress smoothly and will reduce the possibility of injury to the participants. A constant study and review of the rules are also necessary.
2. Prepare yourself both physically and mentally. This will enable you to make quick and positive decisions. It will increase your self-confidence and help to eliminate unnecessary questioning by the contestants.
3. Be firm, but not arrogant; fair, but not officious; and clear and concise, not show-offish in enforcing the rules of play. This will help you to gain the respect of the players, coaches and spectators.
4. Know the duties and responsibilities of your specific assignment, as well as those of the other officials. It may be necessary for you to assume the duties of one of the other officials sometime during a contest.
5. Communicate with both teams through the proper team representative(s).

Do's and Don'ts for Good Officiating

Photograph courtesy of Larry Coffin.

Do not argue with or allow the players to address you indiscriminately. Courteous inquiries during a time-out or when you are not engaged should be answered in the same spirit.

6. Make a concerted effort to develop a basic knowledge and understanding of human nature. This will help you to anticipate and control different situations as they arise.

7. Do not be overly familiar. Be polite in all dealings with players, coaches and team representatives. It not only sets a good example but encourages cooperation among all concerned.

8. Be loyal to the other officials. Do not attempt to shift the blame or publicly criticize the other officials. Avoid discussions regarding your fellow officials and their techniques either on or off the field. Officiating is a *team effort.*

9. Call all fouls regardless of the pressure from the fans, the score, whom it will hurt or how it will affect your future interrelations. Your reputation should be built on the basis of your uncompromising honesty and integrity.

Don'ts

DON'T TAKE YOUR EYES OFF THE PLAY
(Always watch the play, too many officials are spectators)
DON'T TAKE ANYTHING FOR GRANTED
(Always expect anything and everything)
DON'T EXPLAIN DECISIONS
(You are in a no win situation and can only lose, not gain)
DON'T ARGUE WITH PLAYERS OR COACHES
(Even if you win you still lose)
DON'T TALK BACK TO SPECTATORS
(When you start talking to spectators, your name is gone)
DON'T LOOK FOR TROUBLE
(Courtesy and a kind word can save a ball game)
DON'T MAKE DECISIONS FOR YOUR PARTNERS
(Only help when they need help)
DON'T OFFICIATE WITHOUT PROPER EQUIPMENT
(You owe it to yourself, the profession and the game to look your best)
DON'T HOLD IDLE CONVERSATION WITH PLAYERS OR COACHES
(It may be misinterpreted and cause trouble)
DON'T STAND ON A DIME
(Always hustle)
DON'T BLOW YOUR WHISTLE IF YOU DON'T SEE ALL OF THE PLAY
(Guessing is poor officiating)
DON'T IMAGINE OR SUSPECT
(Call only what you see)

Photo courtesy of Carol Harding

CHAPTER III

Uniform and Equipment

When officiating a football game, officials should wear the appropriate uniform that is standard for their school, community or local officials' association. An official's uniform usually consists of a black-and-white striped shirt, white football knickers or dark slacks, dark shoes and a distinctive hat (e.g. black with white stripes). On foul weather days, a white, transparent or black-and-white-striped jacket can also be worn. On many campuses, women officials usually have the option of wearing a dark skirt or shorts.

The uniform should be clean and neat. It should fit properly and allow for freedom of movement. It should not be baggy. A neat tailored appearance gives the impression that the individual cares about his/her appearance, is confident, and knows and understands what officiating is all about. A sloppily dressed or unkept appearance gives the impression that the official is careless, lazy and really does not know or even care about what is going to take place. In addition to a clean and neat uniform, officials should keep their shoes shined to enhance their overall appearance. The initial impression of officials at the start of a contest may make the difference on both how the game is conducted and how the decisions of the officials are received by the players, coaches and spectators.

In addition to his/her uniform, an official should carry three pieces of equipment when officiating a touch and flag football game. This includes a whistle to start and stop play, a flag for marking penalties when they occur and a down indicator to record the down and time-outs. Having the proper equipment not only facilitates the task of officiating but enhances the professional image of the official.

In short, *officials should look and dress like officials.* A clean, neat and properly-fit uniform will make their job a little easier and a lot more enjoyable.

CHAPTER IV

Officiating Procedures and Mechanics

Officials are charged with the responsibility of enforcing and administering all the rules of the game. To efficiently and effectively perform this task, they must work cooperatively and be in the best possible position at all times when making a call.

To help officials accomplish this task and to make the job of officiating a football game a little easier, a system of field and play coverage has been developed. This technique of coverage is commonly referred to as the "mechanics" of officiating. Through the adherence to proper mechanics, officials are able to cover all areas of the field of play or handle the game situation that may arise.

Prior to officiating a contest, officials should learn the proper mechanics of field coverage and the responsibilities and duties of each specific official's position. This can only be accomplished through study and practice. Only through a thorough preparation can officials develop the ability to react automatically to each situation as it occurs.

The mechanics and responsibilities presented in this book apply mainly to officiating crews which utilize three individuals—a referee, an umpire and a linesman. It should be mentioned, however, that if an individual has a thorough knowledge and understanding of the mechanics, duties and responsibilities of football officials, then he/she can adapt, adjust, and modify them to apply to two-, three-, four- and five-person officiating teams.

PRE-GAME MECHANICS AND RESPONSIBILITIES FOR OFFICIALS

A. BEFORE ARRIVAL ON THE FIELD

General — All Officials

1. Notify the management by card verifying the game assignment, the date, the time and the position.
2. Contact the other officials who will assist in officiating the game.
3. Check your own personal officiating equipment and get it ready for the game.
4. Arrive at the game site in plenty of time — at least one hour before the start of the contest.
5. Notify the management of your arrival.
6. Secure the game balls.

Pre-Game Conference — All Officials

1. Review the coin toss mechanics.
2. Review the free-kick positions and responsibilities.
3. Review mechanics and responsibilities on plays from scrimmage including:
   a. running plays.
   b. forward pass plays.
   c. illegal passes
4. Review coverage on kicks from scrimmage.
   a. First touching.
   b. Fair catch.
   c. Interference.
   d. Out-of-Bounds.
5. Review procedures on goal line plays and try-for-points.
6. Review procedures on time-outs and interim periods.
7. Review the first down procedure on zone-to-gain.
8. Review the procedures on administering penalties.
9. Discuss blowing the whistle and dead ball spots.

B. ARRIVAL ON THE FIELD

General — All Officials

1. Arrive on the field of play at least 15 minutes prior to the start of the game.
2. Meet the coaches.
3. Confer with the clock operator and game announcer, if utilized.
4. Inspect the playing field.

The Referee

1. Arranges for the ball boys.
2. Signals the linesman and the umpire to bring the team captains to midfield for the coin toss.

The Linesman

1. Instructs the individual who will work with the down marker.
2. Escorts the home team captain to midfield for the pre-game coin toss after a signal from the referee.

The Umpire
    1. Escorts the visiting team captain to midfield for the pre-game coin toss after a signal from the referee.

C. THE COIN TOSS
Introductions
    1. The linesman and the umpire introduce the team captains to the referee and then assume a position on or about the 35-yard line.
    2. The Referee introduces the team captains to the other officials.

The Toss
    1. The referee flips the coin in the air and lets it drop to the ground.
    2. The visiting team captain calls either heads or tails while the coin is in the air.
    3. The referee places one hand on the shoulder of the winner of the coin toss and offers the following options:
       a. Kick.
       b. Receive.
       c. Choice of goal to defend.
    4. The team captains then assume a position facing the direction of the goal line they will advance towards.
    5. The referee indicates the choice for each team by utilizing a catching or kicking signal.
    6. All the officials record the results of the toss and upon a signal from the referee move to their respective kick-off positions.

SPECIFIC PRE-GAME RESPONSIBILITIES

This section includes an extensive overview of the pre-game duties and responsibilities for the referee, the linesman and the umpire.

A. RESPONSIBILITIES OF THE REFEREE
    I. Obligations
       a. Appear at the contest in plenty of time.
       b. Be prepared both physically and mentally to officiate.

    2. Qualifications
       a. Knowledge and understanding of the rules.
       b. Good physical condition.
       c. Neat and clean personal appearance.
       d. Knowledge and understanding of officiating mechanics.
       e. Ability and willingness to work.
       f. Cooperation with other officials, players and coaches.
       g. Courteous manner.
       h. Courage to make a call.
       i. Good judgment and coolness under fire.
       j. Concentration.
       k. Good sense of humor.
       l. High ethical standards.

3. Pre-Game Procedure
   a. Notify the management of your presence upon arrival at the game site.
   b. Check to see if the other officials are present.
   c. Dress in the proper officiating uniform.
   d. Check the starting time and synchronize your watch.
   e. Secure the game ball from the management.
   f. Hold a pre-game conference with the other officials and discuss:
      1. Position and responsibilities of all officials on and after the kick-off.
      2. Mechanics and responsibilities for
         a. Runs from scrimmage.
         b. Passes from scrimmage.
         c. Kicks from scrimmage.
         d. Goal line plays.
         e. Field goal attempts.
         f. Try-for-points.
         g. Out-of-Bounds coverage.
      3. Discuss any play, rule or game situations that might arise or an official has some concern about.
   g. Check the timing with the clock operator.
4. The Toss
   a. Have all officials present to make them aware of any discussion that takes place.
   b. Introduce the team captains to the other officials.
   c. Ask the team captains if they have any questions relating to the game.
   d. Explain the coin toss procedure.
   e. Flip the coin.
   f. Have the visiting team captain call the coin toss while it is still in the air.
   g. Explain the options to the winner of the toss.
      1. Kick.
      2. Receive.
      3. Select a goal to defend.
   h. Refer to section C, THE COIN TOSS on page 00.

B. RESPONSIBILITIES OF THE LINESMAN
   1. Obligations
      a. Same as those for the referee on page 00.
   2. Qualifications
      a. Same as those for the referee on page 00.
   3. Pre-Game Procedure
      a. Notify the manager of your presence upon arrival at the game site.
      b. Notify the referee of your presence upon arrival.
      c. Dress in the proper officiating uniform.
      d. Participate in the pre-game conference.
      e. Check on uniform and all the equipment that is needed before going to the field.
      f. Take the field with the other officials 15 minutes prior to game time.

4. Field Duties Prior To Start Of Game
   a. Determine which side of the field you will work on.
   b. Arrange for ball boys upon the request of the referee.
   c. Secure and accompany the home team captain to the center of the field for the pre-game coin toss.
   d. Introduce the captain to the referee and then assume a position approximately 5 yards away from the coin toss.
5. Duties Prior To Kick-Off
   a. Check the sideline to make sure it is clear and the teams are in their designated place.
   b. Assume a position opposite the referee at the middle of the field.
   c. Count the players on the receiving team to make sure they have the correct number of players on the field.
   d. Raise the arm above the head to indicate to the referee that you are ready for play.
   e. Refer to officiating procedures for free kicks for additional information.

C. RESPONSIBILITIES OF THE UMPIRE
   1. Obligations
      a. Same as those for the referee on page 00.
   2. Qualifications
      a. Same as those for the referee on page 00.
   3. Pre-Game Procedure
      a. Notify the management of your presence upon arrival at the game site.
      b. Notify the referee of your presence upon arrival.
      c. Dress in the proper officiating uniform.
      d. Participate in the pre-game conference.
      e. Take the field with the other officials 15 minutes prior to game time
   4. Field Duties Prior To Start Of Game
      a. Check both teams for illegal equipment.
      b. Check the end zone flags.
      c. Secure the game ball from the referee.
      d. Assist the referee in the pre-game coin toss.
      e. Secure and accompany the visiting team captain to the center of the field for the pre-game coin toss.
      f. Introduce the captain to the referee and then assume a position approximately 5 yards away from the coin toss.
   5. Duties Prior To Kick-Off
      a. Check the sideline to make sure it is clear and the teams are in their designated place.
      b. Assume a position over the ball on the restraining line of the kicking team.
      c. Count the players on the kicking team to make sure they have the correct number of players on the field.
      d. Raise the arm above the head and signal the referee that the kicking team is ready.
      e. For additional information, refer to officiating procedures for free-kicks.

The next sections provide information pertaining to the mechanics and responsibilities of officials for specific play situations. The following game situations are discussed: free-kicks, running plays, forward pass plays, kicks from scrimmage, goal line plays, field goal attempts and try-for-points. In addition, several other special situations that occur during a game are also covered. These include administration of penalties, actions concerning time outs, and duties of all officials at the end of a period, between quarters, between halves and at the end of a game.

OFFICIATING PROCEDURES ON FREE KICKS

The following procedures are utilized by officials on all free kicks (kick-offs).

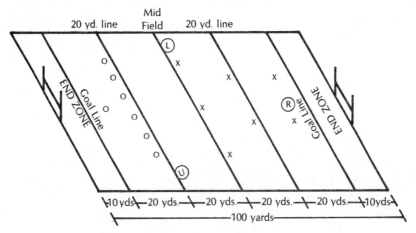

Illustration 1. Position of Officials on a Free Kick.

A. Responsibilities of The Referee

1. Assumes a position in the center of the field near the goal line.
2. Counts the players on the receiving team.
3. Motions the other officials to the sidelines.
4. Raises one arm above the head to request the ready signal from the other officials.
5. Lowers the arm and blows the whistle signaling that everyone is ready for play and to kick the ball.
6. Watches for the ball going out-of-bounds or over the goal line and the end zone.
7. Picks up and trails the ball carrier, if the ball is caught in the field of play.

8. Watches for any infraction of the rules.
9. Gives a blast on the whistle when the ball becomes dead.
10. Spots the ball after the play is whistled dead and proceeds to implement the procedure utilized BEFORE THE SNAP of the ball by the referee on RUNNING PLAYS FROM SCRIMMAGE.

B. Responsibilities of The Linesman

1. Assumes a position facing the receiving team in the middle of the field at the receiving team's restraining line.
2. Counts the players on the receiving team and makes sure at least 3 players are within 5 yards of their restraining line.
3. Makes sure the receiving team is ready to play.
4. Moves to the sideline upon receiving a signal from the referee.
5. Raises and holds one arm above the head when signaling everyone is ready-for-play.
6. Watches at the kick to see that at least 3 players on the receiving team remain within their restraining lines until the ball is kicked.
7. Watches for a short free kick and for first team touching after the ball has traveled 20 yards.
8. Watches for kicks on the same side of the field as positioned.
9. Moves slowly downfield after the kick.
10. Picks up and follows the ball carrier on the same side of the field as positioned if the ball carrier runs to the linesman's side of the field.
11. Watches for any infraction of the rules.
12. Gives a blast on the whistle when the ball becomes dead.
13. Assists the other officials in retrieving and spotting the ball.
14. Proceeds to implement the procedure utilized BEFORE THE SNAP of the ball by the linesman on RUNNING PLAYS FROM SCRIMMAGE.

C. Responsibilties of The Umpire

1. Assumes a position over the ball on the restraining line of the kicking team.
2. Counts the players on the kicking team.
3. Instructs the kicker to wait for the referees ready signal before kicking the ball.
4. Moves to the sideline on the restraining line of the kicking team, opposite the linesman upon a signal from the referee.
5. Raises and holds one arm above the head when signaling everyone is ready-for-play.
6. Watches for offsides on the kicking team on the kick-off.
7. Watches for first touching of the ball by a member of the kicking team before it crosses the receiving team's restraining line or has been touched by a player of the receiving team.
8. Watches for kicks going out-of-bounds on the same side of the field as positioned.
9. Picks up and follows the ball carrier on the same side of the field as positioned if the ball carrier runs to the umpire's side of the field.

10. Watches for any infraction of the rules.
11. Gives a blast on the whistle when the ball becomes dead.
12. Assists the other officials in retrieving and spotting the ball.
13. Proceeds to implement the procedure utilized BEFORE THE SNAP of the ball by the umpire on RUNNING PLAYS FROM SCRIMMAGE.

OFFICIATING PROCEDURES ON RUNNING PLAYS FROM SCRIMMAGE

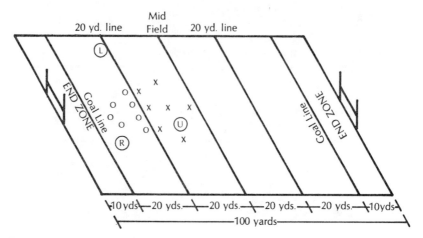

Illustration 2. Position of Officials Prior to the Snap on a Running or Pass Play from Scrimmage.

A. BEFORE THE SNAP
The Referee
1. Spots the ball.
2. Announces the number of the down and the distance to go for a first down.
3. Moves away from the ball and gives the ready-for-play signal accompanied by a blast on the whistle.
4. Moves to a position as deep as the deepest player in the offensive backfield on the opposite side of the linesman.
   a. The exact spot or position will vary according to the type of formation used.
5. Starts and checks the 25-second count until the ball is put into play while moving into position.
6. Watches for illegal motion and illegal shift prior to and at the snap.
7. Watches the legality of the snap. (Before, during and at the snap.)

The Linesman
1. Assists the referee in spotting the ball.
2. Assumes a position on the line of scrimmage relative to the formation being used.

       a. This position is usually 5 to 10 yards outside the defensive end on the linesman's side of the field.

       b. This position should always be outside of all the players on the field, even if it places the linesman on the sidelines.

3. Checks the down marker for correct down and proper alignment with the ball.
4. Watches for illegal procedure prior to the snap.
       a. The offensive line must be totally still for 1 second prior to the snap of the ball.
       b. All the offensive linemen must be within 1 foot of the line of scrimmage.
5. Watches for encroachment, false starts and illegal shifts.
6. Watches and checks the legality of the player going in motion away from the linesman's side of the field.

The Umpire

1. Assists the referee in spotting the ball.
2. Assumes a position in the defensive backfield appropriate to the situation.
       a. This position is usually 10 to 15 yards deep behind the defensive line and between the defensive ends favoring the side opposite the linesman.
       b. The position assumed is such that it will not interfere with the vision or movement of the defensive backs.
3. Watches for illegal procedure and interference prior to the snap.

B. AFTER THE SNAP
The Referee

1. Watches initially for illegal use of the hands at the snap.
2. Watches the ball and the ball carrier and does not rush in too soon after the snap.
3. Does not follow the runner too closely on runs to the linesman's side of the field. The linesman will pick the runner up in that area. The referee then watches the action away from the ball.
4. Trails the runner on a run to the referee's side of the field.
5. Drops a marker and carries out the duties until the play is whistled dead, when a foul is committed. The spot where the foul occurred and where the ball became dead should be noted.
6. Gives a blast on the whistle when the ball becomes dead.
7. Assists in getting the ball to the inbounds spot if no foul has occurred.
8. Signals for a time-out, if a foul, first down, change of possession or any other situation occurs which stops the clock.
9. Gets the complete information when a foul is called by another official and then gives the preliminary signal. (For additional information see section on ADMINISTERING PENALTIES.)
10. Administers the penalty.
11. Spots the ball and then implements the procedure utilized by the referee BEFORE THE SNAP of the ball.

The Linesman

1. Observes the initial charge at the line of scrimmage.
2. Watches for encroachment, illegal procedure, illegal use of hands, holding and other fouls committed near the line of scrimmage.
3. Checks to see if a player going in motion is clearly going lateral or backward.
4. Assists the referee in determining the foremost progress of the ball on runs up the middle. (Signals the referee with one foot thrust slightly forward.)
5. Follows the action slowly watching the play away from the ball on runs to the opposite side of the field. Picks up the ball carrier when a reverse occurs.
6. Retreats as fast as possible and picks up the runner on runs to the linesman's side of the field. If unable to retreat fast enough, moves toward the offensive team's side of the field and then trails the runner downfield.
7. Drops a marker and carries out the duties until the play is whistled dead if a foul occurs. The linesman should note the spot where the foul occurred and where the ball was whistled dead. The foul is then reported to the referee.
8. Gives a sharp blast on the whistle when the ball becomes dead.
9. Assists the other officials in getting the ball to the inbounds spot.
10. Signals the down marker to be moved when the referee so indicates.
11. Signals the number of the down by raising an arm and extending the fingers before each down.
12. Proceeds to perform the procedures utilized by the linesman BEFORE THE SNAP of the ball.

The Umpire

1. Watches initially at the snap for illegal use of hands, holding and other fouls committed near the line of scrimmage.
2. Retreats as fast as possible and picks up the runner on runs to the umpire's side of the field.
3. Follows the play and watches the action away from the ball on runs to the opposite side of the field. Picks up the runner on reverses.
4. Drops a marker and carries out the duties until the play is whistled dead if a foul occurs. The umpire should note the spot where the foul occurred and where the ball is whistled dead. The foul is then reported to the referee.
5. Gives a sharp blast on the whistle when the ball becomes dead.
6. Assists the other officials in getting the ball to the inbounds spot.
7. Signals the number of the down by raising an arm and extending the fingers before each down.
8. Proceeds to perform the procedures utilized by the umpire BEFORE THE SNAP of the ball.

All Officials

1. Work as a team in moving the game along.
2. Keep each play properly boxed in.

3. Sound their whistle when the ball becomes dead.
4. Drop a marker when they see foul occur.
5. Inform the referee when they call a foul. Tell the referee the type of foul committed, the status of the ball and the offending players.
6. Check the correct enforcement of the penalty.
7. Widen and adjust their positions to accomodate the formation being used, especially when a spread formation is employed.
8. Assist in relaying and spotting the ball.
9. Assist in marking the forward progress of the ball.
10. Assist in getting the ball ready for play.

OFFICIATING PROCEDURES ON FORWARD PASS PLAYS

A. BEFORE THE SNAP
The Referee
1. Follows the same procedure utilized for RUNNING PLAYS FROM SCRIMMAGE.

The Linesman
1. Follows the same procedure utilized for RUNNING PLAYS FROM SCRIMMAGE.

The Umpire
1. Follows the same procedure utilized for RUNNING PLAYS FROM SCRIMMAGE INCLUDING:
   a. In obvious passing situations, the umpire assumes a position deeper in the defensive backfield.
   b. The depth of the position may be 10 to 15 yards behind the defensive line.

B. AFTER THE SNAP
The Referee
1. Watches both the ball and the passer.
2. Determines if the pass is either:
   a. forward
   b. lateral
   c. illegal
3. Determines if the passer was behind the line of scrimmage when the ball is released.
4. Observes all blocks behind the line of scrimmage.
5. Watches for roughing the passer.
6. Trails the play on a completed pass.
7. Picks up a breakaway runner on an intercepted pass.
8. Gives the signal on an incompleted pass.
9. Performs other additional duties. SEE PROCEDURES ON RUNNING PLAYS FROM SCRIMMAGE.
10. Spots the ball and then implements the procedures utilized by the referee BEFORE THE SNAP of the ball.

The Linesman

1. Observes the initial line play.
2. Drifts to the outside but stays near the line of scrimmage until the ball is thrown. Then drifts downfield and covers a pass on the linesman's side of the field.
3. Watches for short passes down the middle of the field.
4. Gives the signal on an incompleted pass when in the area of the missed pass.
5. Helps to retrieve the ball.
6. Blows the whistle sharply when the ball becomes dead.
7. Follows the play and observes the action away from it on a completed pass on the opposite side of the field.
8. Observes the runner and covers the sideline to watch for a possible out-of-bounds on a completed pass on the linesman's side of the field.
9. Picks up a breakaway runner if a pass is intercepted.
10. Signals the down marker to be moved when a first down is made and at the request of the referee.
11. Performs other additional duties. SEE PROCEDURES ON RUNNING PLAYS FROM SCRIMMAGE.
12. Assists in spotting the ball and then implements the procedures utilized by the linesman BEFORE THE SNAP of the ball.

The Umpire

1. Observes the initial charge of the line.
2. Watches for any fouls committed on the line of scrimmage.
3. Drops back into the secondary to observe the potential pass receivers.
4. Watches for pass interference both offensive and defensive.
5. Follows the runner closely if the pass is completed.
6. Blows the whistle sharply when the ball becomes dead.
7. Blows the whistle and gives the correct signal when the pass is incomplete.
8. Signals the referee when a first down is made.
9. Performs other additional duties. SEE PROCEDURES ON RUNNING PLAYS FROM SCRIMMAGE.
12. Retrieves and assists in spotting the ball and then implements the procedures utilized by the umpire BEFORE THE SNAP of the ball.

All Officials

1. Follows the same procedure utilized for RUNNING PLAYS FROM SCRIMMAGE *AFTER THE SNAP* of the ball.

OFFICIATING PROCEDURES ON ANNOUNCED KICKS FROM SCRIMMAGE

A. BEFORE THE SNAP

The Referee

1. **Follows the same procedure utilized for RUNNING PLAYS FROM SCRIMMAGE** *INCLUDING:*
   a. Assuming a position near the line of scrimmage about 10 yards to the side of the kicker. This position enables the referee to watch the kicker, the snapper and the line of scrimmage.

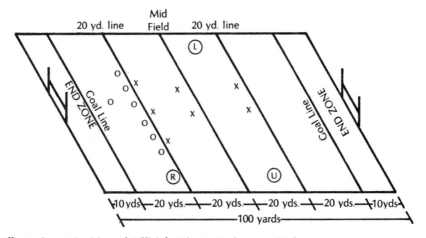

Illustration 3. Position of Officials Prior to Scrimmage Kick

The Linesman

    1. Follows the same procedure utilized for RUNNING PLAYS FROM SCRIMMAGE *INCLUDING:*

      a. Assuming a position opposite the deepest receiver on the linesman's side of the field.

      b. Being responsible for the receiver, the sideline and the goal line on the same side of the field as positioned.

The Umpire

    1. Follows the same procedure utilized for RUNNING PLAYS FROM SCRIMMAGE *INCLUDING:*

      a. Assuming a position opposite the deepest receiver on the linesman's side of the field.

      b. Being responsible for the receiver, the sideline and the goal line on the same side of the field as positioned.

B. AFTER THE SNAP

The Referee

    1. Watches both the ball and the kicker simultaneously until the ball is kicked.

    2. Follows the flight of the ball.

    3. Watches to see if the kicked ball crosses beyond the line of scrimmage.

    4. Trails the play downfield observing the rear action away from the ball.

    5. Picks up the breakaway runner.

    6. Wave the nearest official to the correct spot on the sideline when a ball is kicked out-of-bounds in the air. This official should be lined up with the referee to help insure accuracy.

    7. Gives a blast on the whistle when the ball becomes dead.

    8. Instructs the down marker to be moved as soon as the ball is whistled dead.

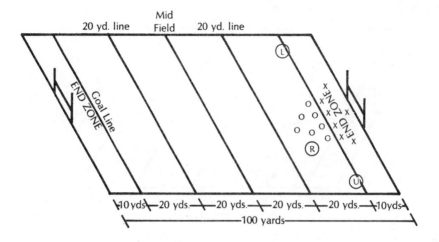

Illustration 4. Position of Officials on Goal Line Plays.

A. BEFORE THE SNAP
The Referee
   1. Follows the same procedure utilized for RUNNING PLAYS FROM SCRIM-
   MAGE.

The Linesman
   1. Follow the same procedure utilized for RUNNING PLAYS FROM SCRIM-
   MAGE *INCLUDING:*
   a. Assuming a position within 5 yards of the widest lineman.

The Umpire
   1. Follows the same procedure utilized for RUNNING PLAYS FROM SCRIM-
   MAGE *INCLUDING:*
   a. Assuming a position on the goal line opposite the linesman and outside
   the End.

B. AFTER THE SNAP
The Referee
   1. Follows the same procedure utilized for RUNNING PLAYS FROM SCRIM-
   MAGE *INCLUDING:*
   a. Observing the play on and behind the line of scrimmage.
   b. Watching for fumbles and change of possession.
   c. Deciding promptly if a touchdown, safety or touchback occurs.
   d. Signaling correctly and promptly what occurs.

The Linesman
   1. Follows the same procedure utilized for RUNNING PLAYS FROM SCRIM-
   MAGE *INCLUDING:*

28

9. Spots and waits over the ball until the down marker is moved and set.
10. Signals first down and the zone-to-gain.
11. Proceeds to implement the procedures utilized by the referee BEFORE THE SNAP of the ball.

The Linesman

1. Follows the flight of the kicked ball.
2. Watches for the fair catch signal and fair catch interference.
3. Watches for a fumble by the receiver.
4. Watches for kicks going out-of-bounds or in the end zone on the linesman's side of the field.
5. Trails the play after the ball is caught.
6. Picks up the runner on the same side of the field as positioned.
7. Follows the play on the runback watching for illegal use of hands, clipping or other fouls.
8. Gives a blast on the whistle when the ball becomes dead.
9. Moves to the sideline spot instructed by the referee if the kicked ball goes out-of-bounds in the air.
10. Marks the spot on the sideline if the kicked ball goes out-of-bounds on the ground and gives a blast on the whistle.
11. Assists the other officials in retrieving and spotting the ball.
12. Signals the down marker to be moved upon notification by the referee.
13. Notifies the referee when the down marker is moved and set in place.
14. Proceeds to implement the procedures utilized by the linesman BEFORE THE SNAP of the ball.

The Umpire

1. Follows the flight of the kicked ball.
2. Watches for the fair catch signal or fair catch interference.
3. Watches for a fumble by the receiver.
4. Watches for kicks going out-of-bounds or in the end zone on the umpire's side of the field.
5. Trails the play after the ball is caught.
6. Picks up the runner on the same side of the field as positioned.
7. Follows the play on the runback watching for illegal use of hands, clipping or other fouls.
8. Gives a blast on the whistle when the ball becomes dead.
9. Moves to the sideline spot instructed by the referee if the kicked ball goes out-of-bounds in the air.
10. Marks the spot on the sideline if the kicked ball goes out-of-bounds on the ground and gives a blast on the whistle.
11. Assists the other officials in retrieving and spotting the ball.
12. Takes a position behind the defense on the opposite side of the linesman and implements the procedures utilized by the umpire BEFORE THE SNAP of the ball.

a. Watching and marking the forward progress of the ball.
b. Watching for fumbles and change of possession.
c. Deciding and signaling promptly and correctly if a touchdown, safety or touchback occurs.
d. Watching the forward progress of the ball and the runner when the run is on the same side as initially positioned.
e. Covering passes on the same side of the field as positioned. Gets out of way of potential receivers by retreating as fast as possible toward the side and end lines.

The Umpire
1. Follows the same procedure utilized for RUNNING PLAYS FROM SCRIMMAGE *INCLUDING:*
a. those duties and responsibilities listed above for the linesman.

OFFICIATING PROCEDURES ON A FIELD GOAL ATTEMPT
A. BEFORE THE SNAP
The Referee
1. Follows the same procedure utilized for RUNNING PLAYS FROM SCRIMMAGE *INCLUDING:*
a. Assuming a position behind the kicker to watch the flight of the ball.

The Linesman
1. Follows the same procedure utilized for RUNNING PLAYS FROM SCRIMMAGE.

The Umpire
1. Follows the same procedure utilized for RUNNING PLAYS FROM SCRIMMAGE *INCLUDING:*
a. Assuming a position on or near the goal posts to watch the flight of the ball.

B. AFTER THE SNAP
The Referee
1. Follows the same procedure utilized for KICKS FROM SCRIMMAGE *INCLUDING:*
a. Judging whether or not the field goal attempt was successful.
*Note - The referee should check with both the linesman and the umpire before giving the correct signal.

The Linesman
1. Follows the same procedure utilized for KICKS FROM SCRIMMAGE *INCLUDING:*
a. Watching for roughing of the kicker and holder.

The Umpire
1. Watches the flight of the ball to see if it goes over the crossbar and through the goal posts.
2. Signals the correct decision to the referee.
3. Watches the ball to see if it crosses the goal line if the field goal is not successful.

4. Prepares to cover a runback if the attempt is unsuccessful and is caught by a player on the defensive team.
5. Blows the whistle sharply when the ball becomes dead.
6. Retrieves the ball and assists in spotting it.
7. Performs other additional duties. SEE PROCEDURES ON KICKS FROM SCRIMMAGE.

OFFICIATING PROCEDURE ON A TRY-FOR-POINT

A. BEFORE THE SNAP

The Referee
1. Spots the ball on the three yard line.
2. Follows the same procedures utilized for GOAL LINE PLAYS when a running or passing play is attempted.
3. Follows the same procedure utilized for a FIELD GOAL ATTEMPT when a kick is tried.

The Linesman and The Umpire
1. Follows the same procedure utilized for GOAL LINE PLAYS when a running or passing play is attempted.
2. Follows the same procedure utilized for a FIELD GOAL ATTEMPT when a kick is tried.

B. AFTER THE SNAP

The Referee, Linesman and Umpire
1. All follow the same procedure utilized for a GOAL LINE PLAY when either a run or a pass is attempted until the ball becmes dead.

OFFICIATING PROCEDURES ON ADMINISTERING PENALTIES

A. WHEN A PENALTY OCCURS

All Officials
1. Drop a penalty marker at the spot of the infraction when they call a foul.
2. Note the player committing the foul and the status and position of the ball at the time of the foul.
3. Continue to follow the play until the ball is whistled dead.
4. Give the time-out signal.

B. WHEN THE BALL BECOMES DEAD

The Official Calling the Infraction
1. Informs the referee immediately of
   a. the nature of the foul.
   b. the offending player and team.
   c. the status and position of the ball at the time of the foul.
2. Stays near the referee to make sure the correct information was received.

The Referee
1. Gives the preliminary signal of the infraction after getting information pertaining to it from the official making the call.
2. Calls the Captains together and explains the options as follows:
   a. A foul has been called on Number _____ of the _____ team.

    b. Then addresses the captain of the offended team and states:
       1. If you take the play, it will be ____ team's ball, ____ down, and ____ yards to go.
       2. If you take the penalty, it will be ____ team's ball, ____ down, and ____ yards to go.
    c. The captain of the offended team then indicates the decision.
   3. Enforces the penalty after hearing the captain's decision by
    a. stepping off the proper yardage
    b. placing the ball down
    c. giving the correct signal for the foul
    d. and then announcing the down and yards to go.

The Linesman

1. Checks the penalty enforcement.
2. Knows the correct down.
3. Watches to see that no attendants come on to the field of play.
4. Retrieves and returns the foul marker to the other official, if nearby.
5. Goes to the yardline where the ball will be put into play for the next down.

The Umpire

1. Secures the ball and hands it to the referee at the spot where the penalty will be measured from.
2. Holds the spot where the penalty was measured from in order to double check the yardage assessment.
3. Moves to a position behind the defensive team in preparation for the following play.

OFFICIATING PROCEDURES FOR TIME-OUTS

A. REQUEST FOR TIME-OUT

All Officials

1. Give the time-out signal.
2. Stop the clock.

B. DURING THE TIME-OUT

The Referee

1. Checks with the umpire for the number of time-outs and the time remaining.
2. Checks with the lineman for the down and the distance-to-gain.
3. Watches for substitutions and illegal communications.
4. Reports the down, the distance, the time-outs and the time remaining to each huddle.
5. Gives the ready-for-play signal after 90 seconds.

The Linesman

1. Assumes a position on the same side of the offensive team's huddle nearest their bench.
2. Watches for substitutions and illegal communications on same side as positioned.
3. Checks the number of players on the offensive team when play resumes.

The Umpire

1. Maintains a position near the ball.
2. Watches for substitutions and illegal communications on same side as positioned.
3. Counts the number of players on the defensive team when play resumes.

All Officials

1. Avoid huddling with other officials unless a conference is necessary.
2. Do not visit with players or coaches unless they request information.

OFFICIATING PROCEDURES FOR END OF PERIODS, BETWEEN QUARTERS AND HALVES AND END OF THE GAME

A. END OF PERIOD

Four Minute Notification (If no Field Clock Available)

The Referee

1. Informs both captains and coaches of the time remaining.
2. No notification is necessary if a field clock is utilized.

The Umpire

1. Notifies the referee when there is approximately four minutes remaining in the second and fourth periods of play.
2. No notification is necessary if a field clock is utilized.

Signal At End of Period

The Referee

1. Responsible for end of period, if facing the clock.
2. Announces end of period, if no gun, by holding the ball overhead with both hands at end of play when time has expired.

The Umpire

1. Notifies the referee when there are about 30 seconds remaining in the game.
2. Signals the referee when time expires and the ball becomes dead.

B. BETWEEN QUARTERS

The Referee

1. Writes down the yardline, the down number, and the distance-to-gain.
2. Confirms the yardline, the down number and the distance-to-gain with the linesman.
3. Measures the distance from the nearest yardline to the foremost point of the ball and estimates the distance from the inbounds line.
4. Spots the ball at the corresponding point on the other half of the field with the directions reversed.

The Linesman

1. Records the yardline, the down number and the distance-to-gain.
2. Goes to the yardline where the ball will be put into play to start the next period.
3. Checks to see if the down marker is okay.

The Umpire

1. Assists the referee in determining the position of the ball at the end of the quarter.
2. Records the yardline, the down number and the distance-to-gain.
3. Watches for and does not allow team attendants to come onto the field.

C. BETWEEN HALVES

The Referee

1. Checks with the other officials to confirm which team lost the pre-game coin toss.
2. Meets with both team captains when they return to the field.
3. Gives the choice of kicking or receiving to the captain who lost the pre-game coin toss.
4. Relays the choices to start the second half of play to the coaches and spectators.

The Linesman

1. Moves to a position at the middle of the field after the second half choices have been made.
2. Follows the same procedures utilized for kick-offs to start the game and after touchdowns.

The Umpire

1. Secures the game ball.
2. Keeps the time during the intermission.
3. Assists in getting the team captains to the referee for the second half choice.
4. Assumes a position in the center of the field.
5. Follows the same procedure utilized for kick-offs to start the game and after touchdowns.

All Officials

1. Assemble for a private conference to discuss and review any problems or situations that have or might occur.
2. Return to the field at least five minutes before the second half is to begin.

D. END OF GAME PROCEDURE

All Officials

1. Secure and provide for the return of all equipment.
2. Leave the field of play together.
3. Neither avoid nor seek contact with either the coaches, players or spectators.
4. Do not make any public statements concerning the game.
5. Report any flagrant irregularities that occurred during the game to the proper authorities.

CHAPTER V

Official National Touch And Flag Football Rules for Men and Women*

*The following rules have been selected from the *Official National Touch and Flag Football Rules for Men and Women*. This includes those rules illustrated in this book. The complete set of rules can be obtained from the Athletic Institute, 200 Castlewood Drive, North Palm Beach, Florida, 33408. This reprint from the official rule book is made by the permission of Mr. Don Bushore, Executive Director.

RULE 1 — THE GAME, FIELD, PLAYERS AND EQUPIMENT

Section 1. General

The Game

ARTICLE 1. The game shall be played between two teams of from seven to eleven players each on a rectangular field and with an official football.

Goal Lines

ARTICLE 2. Goal lines for each team shall be established at opposite ends of the field, and each team shall be allowed opportunities to advance the ball across their opponent's goal line by running, passing, or kicking it.

Winning Team

ARTICLE 3. The teams shall be awarded points for scoring according to rule and, unlesss the game is forfeited, the team having the larger score at the end of the game shall be the winning team.

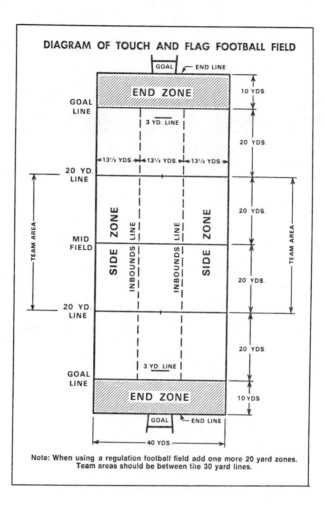

DIAGRAM OF TOUCH AND FLAG FOOTBALL FIELD

Note: When using a regulation football field add one more 20 yard zones.
Team areas should be between the 30 yard lines.

Supervision

ARTICLE 4. The game shall be played under the supervision of either three or four officials: a Referee, Umpire and Linesman (three-man system) or a Referee, Umpire, Linesman and Field Judge (four-man system). Duties of each of the officials can be found in the appendix.

Team Captains

ARTICLE 5. Each team shall designate to the Referee a field captain. The field captain or a designated representative will speak for the team in all dealings with the officials. A field captain's first choice of any option shall be irrevocable.

Persons Subject to the Rules

ARTICLE 6. All players, substitutes, coaches, trainers and other persons affiliated with the team are subject to the rules and shall be governed by the decisions of the officials.

Section 2. The Field

Dimensions

ARTICLE 1. The field shall be a rectangular area with lines and zones as shown in diagram. In case of facility limitations, the length and width of the field can be modified. Note: When teams are composed of more than seven players, a field one hundred twenty yards long with five twenty yard zones and two ten yard end zones is recommended.

Inbounds—Out-of-Bounds

ARTICLE 2. The lines bounding the sidelines and the end zones are out-of-bounds in their entirety, and the inbounds area is bound by those lines. The entire width of each goal shall be a part of the end zone.

Team Area

ARTICLE 3. On each side of the field a team area is designated between the 20 yard lines for the use of the teams, coaches, and authorized team attendants. When the playing area is 120 yards long the team area is between the 30 yard lines.

Goals

ARTICLE 4. Each goal shall consist of two uprights, extended 20 feet above the ground and 23 feet 4 inches apart, measured inside to inside, and no more than 24 feet apart measured outside to outside. The two uprights shall be connected by a horizontal bar, the top of which is 10 feet above the ground. The use of goals is optional.

Pylons

ARTICLE 5. Soft, flexible pylons shall be placed at the inside corners of the four intersections of the goal lines and side lines.

Down Marker

ARTICLE 6. A down marker shall be used to indicate the number of the down.

Obstructions

ARTICLE 7. The Officials of the game should inspect the field and the surrounding area and remove, or order removed, any obstruction which might prove dangerous to players.

Section 3. The Ball

Specifications

ARTICLE 1. The official ball shall be either leather or rubber covered, with two one inch white stripes at either end and shall meet the recommendations for size and shape for regulation football.

Administration

ARTICLE 2. The Referee shall be the sole judge of any ball offered for play and may change the ball during play at his discretion. During the game each team may use a legal ball of its choice when it is in possession.

Section 4. Players and Playing Equipment

ARTICLE 1. For convenience a player is referred to as a linesman or backfieldman.

Contrasting Colors

ARTICLE 2. Players of opposing teams must wear contrasting colors. The referee shall designate which team shall make a change, if necessary.

Equipment

ARTICLE 3. All players should wear regular football jerseys with blocked solid colored numbers contrasting with the jersey on the front and back of the jersey, pants without pads, and rubber-cleated football shoes.

Flags

ARTICLE 4. **Each player on the field will wear a belt at the waistline with two (2) flags attached, but not tied thereto: one flag on each side of the body. Each flag should extend or hang from the waist a minimum of 14 inches. Flags should be 3 inches wide and 16 to 20 inches long. The home team will wear dark colored flags and the visiting team will wear light colored flags. When three flags are used, the third flag should be in the center of the belt in back.**

Wrapping, tying, or in any way securing the flags to the uniform or belt, other than prescribed by rule, or intentionally removing a flag during play, is illegal: *Penalty: 15 yards and possible disqualification.*

Prohibited Equipment

ARTICLE 5. No player wearing illegal equipment shall be permitted to play. The Umpire will decide the legality of all equipment. Illegal equipment shall include:

a. Any equipment which, in the opinion of the Umpire, would confuse or endanger other players.
b. Helmets, padded uniforms, sole leather or other hard or unyielding substance on the hands, wrist, forearms or elbows, no matter how covered or padded.
c. Any projection of metal or other hard substance from a player's person or clothing.
d. Any metal shoe cleats as distinguished from regulation touch football shoes.
e. Jerseys or attachments which tend to conceal the ball by closely resembling it in color.
f. Grease or other slippery substance on a player's person or clothing.
g. Electronic or other signal devices for the purposes of communicating with any outside source.
h. Regulation shoulder pads.

RULE 2—DEFINITIONS

Section 1. The ball: Live, Dead, Loose

Live and Dead Ball

ARTICLE 1. A live ball is a ball in play and a dead ball is a ball not in play. A pass, kick or fumble which has not yet touched the ground is a live ball in flight.

Loose Ball

ARTICLE 3. A loose ball is a live ball. A live ball is always in possession of a team.

When Ball is Ready-for-Play

ARTICLE 3. A dead ball is ready-for-play when the Referee:
a. If time is in, sounds the whistle and signals "ready-for-play."
b. If time is out, sounds the whistle and signals either "start the clock" or "ball ready-for-play."

In Possession

ARTICLE 4. "In Possession" is an abbreviation meaning "in possession of a live ball." A player is in possession when both holding and controlling the ball. A team is in possession: when one of its players is in possession; while a punt, drop kick, or place kick is being attempted; while a forward pass thrown by one of its players is in flight, or during a fumble, backward pass, or illegal forward pass.

Catch, Interception, Recovery

ARTICLE 5. A catch is an act of establishing player-possession of a live ball in flight. A catch of an opponent's pass or fumble before it hits the ground is an interception. Securing possession of a live ball after it strikes the ground is "recovering" it. If a player attempts a catch, interception, or recovery while in the air the ball must be in control when the player returns to the ground inbounds.

Section 2. Blocking

ARTICLE 1. Blocking is legally obstructing an opponent by contacting the opponent with any part of the blocker's body. Blockers must be on their feet before, during, and after contact is made with an opponent. Two on one blocking shall be limited to the area on and behind the neutral zone. Under no condition shall a high-low or rolling block be permitted.

Blocker is allowed to contact only that portion of the opponent's body between the waist and shoulders. Exception: A blocker who loses personal body control due to an opponent's aggressiveness after contact shall not be penalized.

Contact with an opponent may occur only between the opponent's waist and neck. When using a hand or forearm block, the elbow must be entirely outside the shoulder. The blocker's hands may not be blocked. The blocker may not swing, throw, or flip the elbow or forearm. The hands may be closed or cupped but the palms may not be facing the opponent being blocked.

Section 3. Clipping

ARTICLE 1. Clipping is running or diving into the back, or throwing or dropping the body across the back of the leg or legs of an opponent.

Section 4. Down and Between Downs.

ARTICLE 1. A down is a unit of the game which starts, after the ball is ready-for-play, with a snap or free kick and ends when the ball next becomes dead. Between downs is the interval during which the ball is dead.

ARTICLE 2. A down will be played if the whistle is sounded inadvertently during a kick or while a forward pass is in flight.

ARTICLE 3. Encroachment is a term indicating a player is illegally in the neutral zone.

Section 5. Fair Catch

ARTICLE 1. A fair catch is a catch of a kick, which is beyond the neutral zone, by a player of the receiving team, who has signalled their intention by extending one arm and hand only above the head and waving the hand from side to side of the body more than once.

Section 6. Foul and Violation

ARTICLE 1. A foul is a rule infraction for which a penalty is prescribed. A violation is a rule infraction for which no penalty is prescribed and which does not offset the penalty for a foul.

Section 7. Fumble — Muff — Batting — Touching Ball

Fumble

ARTICLE 1. A fumble is loss of player possession other than by handing, pasing or kicking the ball.

Muff

ARTICLE 2. A muff is an unsuccessful attempt to catch or recover a ball, the ball being touched in the attempt.

Batting

ARTICLE 3. Batting the ball is striking it with a hand or arm.

Touching Ball

ARTICLE 4. Touching the ball denotes any contact with it.

Section 8. Goal Lines

ARTICLE 1. Each goal line is a vertical plane separating an end zone from the field of play.

Section 9. Handing the Ball

ARTICLE 1. Handing the ball is transferring player-possession from one teammate to another without throwing, fumbling or kicking it.

Section 10. Huddle

ARTICLE 1. A huddle is two or more offensive players grouped together after the ball is ready for play and before assuming scrimmage formation prior to the snap.

Section 11. Hurdling

ARTICLE 1. Hurdling is an attempt by the runner to jump with both feet foremost over any player(s) still on their feet.

Section 12. Kicks

Legal and Illegal Kicks

ARTICLE 1. A legal kick is a punt, drop kick or place kick by a player of the team in possession when such kick is permitted by rule. Kicking the ball in any other manner is illegal. Any kick continues to be a kick until it is caught or recovered by a player or becomes dead.

Punt

ARTICLE 2. A punt is kicking the ball by the player who drops it and kicks it before it strikes the ground.

Drop Kick

ARTICLE 3. A drop kick is kicking the ball by the player who drops it and kicks it as it touches the ground or as it is rising from the ground.

Place Kick

ARTICLE 4. A place kick is kicking the ball from a fixed position either on the ground or on a tee. The ball may be held in possession by any player of the kicking team. If a tee is used, it may not elevate the ball's lowest point more than two inches above the ground.

Free Kick

ARTICLE 5. A free kick is a kick made under restrictions which prohibit either team from advancing beyond established restraining lines until the ball is kicked.

Kickoff

ARTICLE 6. A kickoff is a free kick which starts each half and follows each try-for-point, safety, or field goal and must be a place kick or a drop kick.

Scrimmage Kick

ARTICLE 7. A scrimmage kick is a kick by Team A during a scrimmage down before team possession changes. It is made under restrictions which prohibit either team from advancing beyond established scrimmage lines until the ball is kicked.

Section 13. Loss of a Down

ARTICLE 1. "Loss of a Down" is an abbreviation meaning: "loss of the right to repeat a down."

Section 14. The Neutral Zone

ARTICLE 1. The neutral zone is the space between the two free kick lines during a free kick and between the two lines of scrimmage during a scrimmage down and is established when the ball is ready for play.

Section 15. Encroachment

ARTICLE 1. Encroachment denotes the position of a player, except that Snapper or the kicker and holder of a place kick for a free kick, any part of whose person is beyond their scrimmage line or their restraining line when the ball is put in play.

Section 16. Passes

Passing

ARTICLE 1. Passing the ball is throwing it. A pass continues to be a pass until caught, intercepted, or the ball becomes dead.

Forward and Backward Pass

ARTICLE 2. A forward pass is a live ball thrown toward the opponent's line. A backward pass is a live ball thrown toward or parallel to the Passer's end line. A pass continues to be a pass until it is caught or recovered by a player or becmomes dead.

Section 17. Penalty

ARTICLE 1. A penalty is a loss imposed by rule upon a team which has committed a foul.

Section 18. Removing the Flag

ARTICLE 1. **When the flag is cleanly taken from a ball carrier the down shall end and the ball is declared dead. A player who removes the flag from the ball carrier should immediately hold the flag above his head to assist the official in locating the spot where the capture occurred.**

ARTICLE 2. **In an attempt to remove a flag from a ball carrier, defensive players may contact the body and shoulders of an opponent with their hands, but not their face or any part of their head. A defensive player may not hold, push, or knock the ball carrier down in any attempt to remove the flag.** *Penalty: 15 yards.*

ARTICLE 3. **The flag may be dropped at the spot of capture by the defense with no penalty.**

Section 19. Scrimmage

Scrimmage

ARTICLE 1. A scrimmage is the interplay of the two teams during a down in which play begins with a snap.

Scrimmage Line

ARTICLE 2. The scrimmage line for each team is the yard-line and its vertical plane which passes through the point of the ball nearest its own goal line. An offensive player is on the line of scrimmage when facing the opponent's goal line with the line of the shoulders approximately parallel to the scrimmage line and with the head breaking the plane of an imaginary line drawn through the waistline of the snapper and parallel to the line of scrimmage.

Stance

ARTICLE 3. All players on both the offense and the defense, except the Snapper, must be on their feet with neither hand touching the ground at the snap. Player's hands on their knees is permissible.

Backfield Line

ARTICLE 4. The backfield line is a vertical plane one yard behind and parallel to the scrimmage line of the offensive team.

Section 20. Shift

ARTICLE 1. A shift is a simultaneous change of position by two or more offensive players after the ball is ready-for-play for a scrimmage and before the next snap.

Section 21. Snapping the Ball

ARTICLE 1. Snapping the ball (a snap) is handing or passing it back from the position on the ground. In a legal snap, the movement must be a quick and continuous motion of the hand or hands during which the ball actually leaves the hand or hands. The ball may not be raised to more than a 45 degree angle at the snap and the long axis of the ball must be at right angles to the scrimmage line.

Section 22. Spots

Enforcement Spot

ARTICLE 1. An enforcement spot is the point from which the penalty for a foul is enforced.

Previous Spot

ARTICLE 2. The previous spot is the point from which the ball was last put in play.

Succeeding Spot

ARTICLE 3. The succeeding spot, as related to a foul, is the point at which the ball would have been put in play if that foul had not occurred.

Dead Ball Spot

ARTICLE 5. The spot of the foul is the point at which that foul occurs. If out-of-bounds between the goal lines it shall be the intersection of the nearer inbounds line and the yard-line, extended, through the spot of the foul.

Out-of-Bounds Spot

ARTICLE 6. The out-of-bounds spot is the point at which the ball becomes dead because of going or being declared out-of-bounds.

Inbounds Spot

ARTICLE 7. The inbounds spot is the intersection of the nearer inbounds line and the yard-line passing through the dead ball spot, or the spot where the ball is left in a side zone by a penalty.

Section 23. Team and Player Designations

Offensive and Defensive Team

ARTICLE 1. The offensive Team (Team A) is the team in possession, or the team to which the ball belongs—the Defensive Team (Team B) is the opposing team.

Kicker

ARTICLE 2. The Kicker is any player who makes a punt, drop kick or place kick.

Lineman and Backfieldman

ARTICLE 3. A lineman is any player on his scrimmage line when the ball is snapped; a back is any player who is at least one yard behind the line when the ball is snapped.

Passer

ARTICLE 4. The passer is the player who has thrown a legal forward pass. He remains the passer while the ball is in flight.

Player

ARTICLE 5. A player is any one of the participants in the game.

Ball Carrier

ARTICLE 6. The Ball Carrier is a player in possession of a live ball.

Snapper

ARTICLE 7. The Snapper is the player who snaps the ball.

Substitute

ARTICLE 8. A substitute is a replacement for a player or a player vacancy.

Disqualified Player

ARTICLE 9. A disqualified player is one who becomes ineligible for further participation in the game.

Section 24. Touching

ARTICLE 1. Touching is the placing of one or both hands anywhere between the shoulders and knees of an opponent with the ball. The foot of the toucher must be in contact with the ground throughout the touch. Pushing, striking, and slapping are not permitted. *Penalty: 15 yards.*

Section 25. Tripping

ARTICLE 1. Tripping is using the lower leg or foot to obstruct an opponent (including the ball carrier) below the knee. *Penalty: 15 yards.*

Section 26. Yardline

ARTICLE 1. A yardline is a line in the field of play parallel to the end line between the goal lines.

Section 27. Deflagging

ARTICLE 1. **Deflagging is the legal removal of a flag of an opponent in possession of the ball. A foot of the deflagger must be in contact with the ground throughout the deflagging. Pushing, striking, holding, or slapping are not permitted.** *Penalty: 15 yards.*

RULE 3—PERIODS, TIME FACTORS, SUBSTITUTES

Section 1. The Start Of Each Period

First and Third Periods

ARTICLE 1. Each half shall start with a kickoff. Three minutes before the start of the game, the Referee shall toss a coin in the presence of the opposing Field Captians, after first designating which Captain shall call the fall of the coin.

a. The Captain winning the toss shall choose one of the following options:
    1. To kick off.
    2. To receive.
    3. To designate which goal his team will defend.
b. The loser of the toss shall make a choice of the remaining option.
c. Before the start of the second half the choosing of options will be reversed.

Second and Fourth Periods

ARTICLE 2. Between the first and second periods and between the third and fourth periods the teams shall exchange goals and the ball shall be relocated in a spot corresponding to its location at the end of the previous period. Possessions of the ball and the down and distance to be gained shall remain the same.

Section 2. Playing Time and Intermissions

Game Time

ARTICLE 1. Playing time shall be of 48 minutes duration, divided into four quarters of twelve minutes each with one minute between the first and second and third and fourth quarters and ten minutes between the second and third quarters. In case of a tie there shall be a one minute intermission before the start of each overtime period.

Shortening Periods

ARTICLE 2. Before the start of the game, playing time may be shortened by mutual agreement of the field captains and the Referee, if darkness threatens. Anytime during the game, the playing time of any remaining period or periods may be shortened by mutual agreement of the opposing captains and the Referee.

Extension of Periods

ARTICLE 3. No period shall end until the ball is dead, and in the case of a touchdown the try-for-point shall be attempted. If playing time for a period expires before completion of the penalty for a foul by Team B while the ball is ready-for-play, or during a down in which Team B commits a foul while Team A is in possession, the period shall be extended until a down which is free from such foul has been played. If Team A commits a foul, or if both teams commit fouls, the period is not extended.

Tie Game

ARTICLE 4. When a game ends in a tie score the two field captains shall be brought together for a coin flip to determine which team shall make the first play and the direction which play shall begin. The winner of the toss selects the first of these options with the loser making the remaining choice. Starting in the center of the field a series of eight alternating downs are played with the team ending in the opponents territory being credited with one point. In case of a touchdown the try for point is attempted and the ball is returned to midfield and given to the team whose turn it is at the time. If the ball ends up at midfield at the end of the eight alternating plays with no score or the score tied, a one minute intermission is taken and the overtime procedure is repeated except that a series of only four alternating plays are made. If necessary, the four alternating plays are repeated until a winner is determined. "Note: If a player of the defensive team intercepts a legal forward pass, the next play will begin at the spot where the ball becomes dead at the end of the run following the interception. Any loss or gain of distance as a result of the interception shall stand and any touchdown scored will count. The ball will next be put in play by the team who would have put the ball in play if the interception had not occurred."

Game Clock

ARTICLE 5. Playing time shall be kept on a stop watch operated by an official or on a field clock operated by a designated timer.

When Clock Starts

ARTICLE 6. Following a free kick the game clock shall be started when the ball is legally touched. On a scrimmage down the game clock shall be started when the ball is snapped or on prior signal by the referee. The clock shall not run during a try-for-point or during an extension of a period.

a. The Referee shall signal and the game clock starts when the ball is ready-for-play, if it was stopped:
   1. By a team time-out, a touchback, an incomplete forward pass, or a live ball going out of bounds; or after a fair catch.
   2. To complete a penalty;
   3. To award a first down;
   4. After both teams are ready, following a change of possession;
   5. At the Referee's discretion.
b. The Referee does NOT signal and the game clock starts when the ball is put in play, if it was stopped:
   1. By a team time-out, a touchback, an incompleted forward pass, or a live ball going out of bounds; or after a fair catch.
c. If incidents in (a), above, occur in conjunction with a free time-out or any other incident following which the clock would not start until the ball is put into play it shall be started when the ball is put in play.

When Clock Stops

ARTICLE 7. The game clock shall be stopped and time is out when each period ends and whenever "time out" is declared by the Referee as in: a touchdown, touchback, field goal, safety, penalty, free time out, out of bounds, or referee's discretion.

Four Minute Warning

ARTICLE 8. Approximately four minutes before each half ends the Referee shall inform each Field Captain and Coach of the playing time remaining in that half. He may order the clock stopped for that purpose if necessary. If a field clock is the official timepiece, notification is not required.

Section 3. Time-Outs

How Charged

ARTICLE 1. The Referee shall declare a time-out when he suspends play for any reason. Each time-out shall be charged either to the Referee or to one of the teams.

Referee's Time-Out

ARTICLE 2. The Referee shall declare an official's time-out whenever a touchdown, field goal, touchback, or safety is made; when an excess time-out is allowed; when the game clock is stopped to complete a penalty; when a forward pass becomes incomplete; and when a live ball goes out-of-bounds.

Discretionary Time-Out

ARTICLE 3. The Referee may declare an official's time-out for any contingency not elsewhere covered by the rules. If a time-out is for repair or replacement of player equipment which became illegal through play and is considered dangerous to other players, the Referee shall charge himself; otherwise he shall charge the team whose player is wearing the illegal equipment. The Referee shall charge himself when an injured player is designated and removed for at least one down.

Free Time-Outs

ARTICLE 4. Each team is entitled to three free time-outs during each half without penalty. Successive free time-outs may be granted each team during a dead ball period. If the ball is dead and a team has not exhausted its free time-outs the Referee shall allow a free time-out and charge the team.

Official's Time-Out

ARTICLE 5. After a team's three time-outs have been exhausted, subsequent requests by its Field Captian may be allowed only for the benefit of a designatd injured player who must leave the game for at least one scrimmage down. Such time-out, if allowed, is an official time-out.

Length of Time-Outs

ARTICLE 6. A free time-out requested by the Field Captain shall not exceed 1½ minutes. Other time-outs shall be no longer than the Referee deems necessary to fulfill the purpose for which they are declared, but any time-out may be extended by the Referee for the benefit of a seriously injured player.

Warning and Notification

ARTICLE 7. The Referee shall warn both teams 30 seconds before a free time-out expires and five seconds later shall declare the ball ready-for-play. When the legal time-outs have been charged to a team in the same half, the Referee shall notify the Field Captain and the Coach of that team.

Sideline Conference

ARTICLE 8. During a time-out charged to a team, one player at a time may confer with the coaching staff at the sideline near the team area.

Section 4. Delays

Delaying the Start of a Half

ARTICLE 1. Each team shall have its players on the field for the opening play at the scheduled time for the beginning of each half. **All players must have their flags in legal position.** *Penalty: 15 yards.*

Illegal Delay of the Game

ARTICLE 2. The ball must be put in play promptly and legally, and any action or inaction by either team which tends to prevent this is illegal delay of the game. This includes:
a. Consuming more than 25 seconds in putting the ball in play after it is ready-for-play.
b. Failing to remove an injured player for whose benefit an officials time-out has been granted.
c. Deliberately advancing the ball after it has been declared dead.
Penalty: For delay of game—5 yards

Unfair Tactics

ARTICLE 3. The Referee may order the game clock started or stopped whenever, in his opinion, either team is trying to conserve or consume playing time by tactics obviously unfair. *Penalty: 5 yards.*

Section 5. Substitutions

Eligible Substitutes

ARTICLE 1. No substitutes shall enter during a down. Between downs any number of eligible substitutes may replace players provided the substitution is completed by having the replaced players off the field before the ball comes alive. An incoming substitute must enter the field directly from his team area. A replaced player must leave at the sideline nearest his team area. *Penalty: 5 yards.*

Legal Substitutions

ARTICLE 2. During the same dead ball interval, no subsitute shall become a player and then withdraw and no player shall withdraw and then re-enter as a substitute.

ARTICLE 3. **Each substitute shall be in uniform, ready for play, with Flags in position as directed in Rule 1, Section 4, Article 4.** *Penalty: 5 yards.*

RULE 4—BALL IN PLAY, DEAD BALL, OUT-OF-BOUNDS

Section 1. Ball in Play — Dead Ball

Dead Ball Becomes Alive

ARTICLE 1. A dead ball, after having been declared ready-for-play, becomes a live ball when it is snapped or free kicked, legally, or illegally.

Live Ball Becomes Dead

ARTICLE 2. A live ball becomes a dead ball as provided in the rules or when an official sounds his whistle (even though inadvertently), or otherwise declares the ball dead.

Ball Declared Dead

ARTICLE 3. A live ball becomes dead and an official shall sound the whistle or declare it dead:

a. When it goes out-of-bounds or when it touches the goal line (vertical plane) of the Ball Carrier's opponents.

b. When any part of the Ball Carrier's person other than a hand or foot touches the ground. *Exception:* The ball remains alive when it will ostensibly be held, or is held, for a kick; it then may be kicked, passed or advanced.

c. When a touchdown, touchback, safety, field goal or successful try-for-point is made.

d. When, during a try-for-point, Team B obtains possession of the ball or when it becomes certain a try-for-point kick will not score the point.

e. When a player of the kicking team catches or recovers any free kick or a scrimmage kick which is beyond the neutral zone; when a free kick or an untouched scrimmage kick comes to rest on the ground and no player attempts to secure it.

f. When a forward pass strikes the ground or is caught simultaneously by opposing players.

g. When a backward pass or fumble by a player touches the ground. *Note: A ball snapped from scrimmage, which hits the ground before or after getting to the intended receiver, is dead at the spot at which it hits the ground.*

h. When a legal forward pass is legally completed, or a loose ball is caught or recovered by a player on, above, or behind the opponent's goal line.

i. When a Ball Carrier is legally touched between the shoulders and knees, including the hand and arm.

j. **When a Ball Carrier has a flag removed legally by a defensive player.**

k. A muff of a kicked ball is dead when it strikes the ground.

l. Following a valid fair catch signal when the kick is caught or recovered between the goal lines by any receiver beyond K's line (unless the kick has been touched by one of the kickers beyond the line).

m. When an official sounds the whistle (even if inadvertently).

If there were an inadvertent whistle during a down which ended behind A's line-of-scrimmage or during a kick or while a legal forward pass or snap was in flight, the down will be replayed unless there was a change of team possession prior to the whistle.

If the whistle were inadvertently sounded while the ball was in player possession, the ball is dead at that point and the down is counted.

If the whistle were inadvertently sounded while the ball was in player possession beyond the line-of-scrimmage, or following a change of team possession, the ball is dead at that point and the down is counted.

If the whistle were inadvertently sounded while the ball was loose following a backward pass or fumble beyond A's line-of-scrimmage or following a change of team possession behind the line, the ball will be awarded to the team last in possession at the spot where possession was lost and the down counted.

Ready For Play

ARTICLE 4. No player shall put the ball in play until it is declared ready-for-play. *Penalty: 5 yards.*

25-Second Count

ARTICLE 5. The ball shall be put in play within 25 seconds after it is declared ready-for-play, unless, during that interval, play is suspended by the Referee. *Penalty: 5 yards.*

Section 2. Out-Of-Bounds

Player or Held Ball Out-of-Bounds

ARTICLE 1. A player is out-of-bounds when any part of that player touches anything other than another player or a game official which is on or outside a boundary line. A ball in player-possession is out-of-bounds when either the ball or any part of the runner touches the ground or anything else, except a player or game official, which is on or outside a boundary line.

Ball Out-of-Bounds

ARTICLE 2. A loose ball (other than a kick which scores a goal) or a forward pass is out-of-bounds when it touches the ground, a player or anything else which is on or outside a boundary line.

Out-of-Bounds at Crossing Point

ARTICLE 3. If a live ball crosses a boundary line and then is declared out-of-bounds it is out-of-bounds at the crossing point.

Out-of-Bounds at Forward Point

ARTICLE 4. If a live ball is declared out-of-bounds because of contact with a player or anything else, and the ball does not cross a boundary line, it is out-of-bounds at the ball's most forward point when it was declared dead.

RULE 5— SERIES OF DOWNS AND ZONE-TO-GAIN

Section 1. A Series— How Started— How Broken— Renewed

A Down is a Unit

ARTICLE 1. A down is a unit of the game which starts with a snap or free kick, and ends when the ball next becomes dead. Between downs is any period when the ball is dead.

Series of Downs

ARTICLE 2. A team, in possession of the ball, shall have four consecutive downs to advance to the next zone by scrimmage. Any down may be repeated if provided for by the rules.

Zone Line To Gain

ARTICLE 3. The line to gain in any series shall be the zone in advance of the ball, unless distance has been lost due to penalty or failure to gain. In such case, the original zone in advance of the ball at the beginning of the series of downs is the line to gain. The most forward point of the ball, when declared dead between the goal lines, shall be the determining factor.

Measurement of Distance

ARTICLE 4. The most forward point of the ball when declared dead between the goal lines shall be the determining point in establishing distance gained or lost by either team in a down.

Awarding A New Series

ARTICLE 5. A new series of downs shall be awarded when a team moves the ball into the next zone on a play free from penalty; or a penalty against the opponents or they have obtained legal possession of a ball as a result of a penalty, free kick, kick from scrimmage, touchbacks, pass interference or failure to gain the zone in advance of the ball.

Section 2. Down and Possession After a Penalty

Foul During Free Kick

ARTICLE 1. When a scrimmage follows the penalty for a foul committed during a free kick, the down and distance established by that penalty shall be first down with next zone to gain.

Penalty Resulting in First Down

ARTICLE 2. After a penalty which leaves the ball in possession of Team A beyond its line-to-gain, or when a penalty stipulates a first down, the down and distance established by that penalty shall be first down with next zone to gain.

Foul Before Change of Team Possession

ARTICLE 3. After a distance penalty between the goal lines incurred during a down and before any change of team possession during that down, the ball belongs to Team A and the down shall be repeated unless the penalty also involves loss of a down, or leaves the ball on or beyond the zone line-to-gain. If the penalty involves loss of a down, the down shall count as one of the four in that series.

Foul After Change of Team Possession

ARTICLE 4. After a distance penalty for a foul committed during a down and after team possession has changed during that down, the ball belongs to the team in possession when the foul occurred and the down and distance established by that penalty shall be first down with zone to gain.

Penalty Declined

ARTICLE 5. If a penalty is declined the number of the next down shall be whatever it would have been if that foul had not occurred.

Foul Between Downs

ARTICLE 6. After a distance penalty incurred between downs, the number of the next down shall be the same as that established before the foul occurred unless enforcement for a foul by Team B leaves the ball on or beyond the zone line-to-gain.

Foul Between Series

ARTICLE 7. A scrimmage following a penalty incurred after a series ends and before the next series begins shall be first down but the zone line-to-gain shall be established before the penalty is enforced.

Fouls by Both Teams

ARTICLE 8. If offsetting fouls occur during a down, or while the ball is ready-for-play for such down, that down shall be repeated. If each offsetting foul occurs between successive downs, the next down shall be the same as it would have been had no fouls occurred. Exception: If there is a change of team possession during a down or at the end of a down, the team last gaining possession may decline offsetting fouls and retain possession after completion of the penalty for its infraction providing that a team had not fouled prior to possession. If each team fouls during a down in which there is a change of team possession, the team last gaining possession may retain the ball, provided its foul was not prior to the final change of possession and it declined the penalty for its opponents foul.

RULE 6—KICKS

Section 1. Free Kicks

Putting the Ball in Play

ARTICLE 1. A free kick begins each half of a game, and begins play following a touchdown, field goal, or safety. The ball shall be put in play by a place kick or a drop kick from some spot on or behind the kicker's restraining line and between the inbounds lines. Unless relocated by penalty the kicking team's restraining line on kickoffs shall be its 20-yard line on fields 100 yards long and the 40 yard line on fields 120 yards long.

Formation

ARTICLE 2. When the ball is legally kicked, all players of the kicking team must be inbounds and all players, except the holder and kicker of a place kick, must be behind their restraining line. At least three players of the receiving team with 7 players, four with 9 players, and five with 11 players must be within five yards of their restraining line after the ball is ready for play and until the ball is kicked. *Penalty: 5 yards.*

Restraining Lines

ARTICLE 3. For any free kick formation the kicking team's restraining line shall be the yard-line through the forward-most point from which the ball may be kicked. The receiving team's restraining line shall be the yard line *twenty yards* beyond that point. It is enroachment for any player other than the kicker and the holder to be beyond the free kick line after the ball is ready for play and until it is kicked.

Recovery of a Free Kick

ARTICLE 4. No player of the kicking team shall touch a free kick before it reaches the receiver's restraining line. Thereafter, all players of the kicking team become eligible to touch, recover, or catch the kick. However, no player of the kicking team may interfere with the receiving team's opportunity to catch the ball. A free kick touched by a player of the kicking team which then touches the ground is dead at the spot at which it touches the ground. If first touched before reaching the restraining line of the receiving team, it belongs to the receiving team. If first touched after reaching the restraining line of the receiving team, the ball belongs to the kicking team. A free kick touched by a player of the receiving team, which then touches the ground, is dead at the spot at which it touches the ground and belongs to the receiving team.

Free Kick Caught or Recovered

ARTICLE 5. If a free kick is caught or recovered by a player of the receiving team, the ball continues in play; If caught or recovered by the kicking team, the ball becomes dead.

Free Kick At Rest

ARTICLE 6. If a free kick inbounds comes to rest and no player of either team attempts to secure it, the ball becomes dead and belongs to the receiving team at the dead ball spot.

Section 2. Free Kick Out-of-Bounds

Out-Of-Bounds Untouched Between the Restraining Lines

ARTICLE 1. If a free kick goes out-of-bounds untouched between the restraining lines, the receiving team will put the ball in play on the inbound spot on the line opposite the out-of-bounds spot.

Out-Of-Bounds Untouched Beyond the Restraining Lines
and Between the Goal Lines

ARTICLE 2. If a free kick goes out-of-bounds untouched beyond the receiving team's restraining line, but between the goal lines, the ball is put in play at the receiving team's restraining line.

Out-of-Bounds Touched Between the Goal Lines

ARTICLE 3. If a free kick, which is touched by either team, goes out-of-bounds before touching the ground after being touched between the goal lines, the ball belongs to the receiving team at the inbounds spot on the line opposite the out-of-bounds spot.

Out-of-Bounds Behind Goal Line

ARTICLE 4. If a free kick goes out-of-bounds behind a goal line, it is a touchback and the ball belongs to the team defending that goal line at their 20-yard line.

Section 3. Scrimmage Kicks

Legal Kick

ARTICLE 1. A legal scrimmage kick is a punt, drop kick or place kick made in accordance with the rules.

Protection on Scrimmage Kicks

ARTICLE 2. When a scrimmage kick is to be made, the kicking team must announce it to the referee before the ball is declared ready-for-play. After such an announcement, the kick must be attempted. (optional)

ARTICLE 3. Until the kick is made, both teams must maintain at least 3 players on the line of scrimmage in 7 players. 4 in 8 or 9 players; and 5 in eleven players. *Penalty: 5 yards. Illegal procedure.*

Kicking the Ball

ARTICLE 4. The kicker must be at least 5 yards behind the line of scrimmage when receiving the snap. After receiving the snap, the kicker must kick the ball immediately and in a continuous motion. *Penalty: Delay—5 yards. If repeated, Unsportsmanlike conduct—15 yards and loss of down.*
Note: Some teams may wish to play with no protection or announcement on scrimmage kicks. When exercising this option, any contact with the kicker results in a penalty. *Penalties: Roughing the kicker-15 yards.*

Failure to Cross the Neutral Zone

ARTICLE 5. Except on a try-for-point, a scrimmage kick which fails to cross the scrimmage line continues in play and all players are eligible to catch or recover the ball and advance it.

Crossing the Neutral Zone

ARTICLE 6. No player of the kicking team shall touch a scrimmage kick which goes beyond the neutral zone before it touches an opponent. Such illegal touching is a violation which gives the receiving team the option of taking the ball at the spot of the touching when the ball becomes dead. However, if a penalty incurred by either team before or as the ball becomes dead is accepted, the option is cancelled.

All Players Become Eligible

ARTICLE 7. When a scrimmage kick which has crossed the neutral zone touches a player of the receiving team, any player may catch the ball.

Spot of First Touching

ARTICLE 8. A scrimmage kick which touches a player of either team and then touches the ground is dead at the spot of touching the ground and belongs to the receiving team at that spot, or at the spot of first touching by the kicking team.

Forced Touching Disregarded

ARTICLE 10. If a scrimmage kick is caught, or recovered after hitting the ground, by a player of the receiving team, the ball continues in play. *Note: If muffed, it becomes dead at the spot of hitting the ground after being muffed.*

Catch Or Recovery By Kicking Team

ARTICLE 11. If a player of the kicking team who is beyond the neutral zone catches or recovers a scrimmage kick, the ball becomes dead and belongs to the receiving team.

Kick Out-Of-Bounds Between the Goal Lines Or At Rest

ARTICLE 12. If a scrimmage kick goes out-of-bounds between the goal lines or comes to rest inbounds untouched and no player attempts to secure it, the ball becomes dead and belongs to the receiving team at that spot.

Kick Out-of-Bounds Behind the Goal LIne

ARTICLE 13. When any kick (other than a successful field goal or try) touches anything while the kicked ball is on or behind the receiver's goal line (plane), it is dead immediately and is a touchback.

Section 4. Opportunity to Catch a Kick

Interference With Opportunity

ARTICLE 1. A player of the receiving team who is so located that he could catch: (1) a free kick or, (2) a scrimmage kick which is beyond the neutral zone and in flight, must be given an unencumbered opportunity to catch such a kick. Protection terminates when the kick is touched by any player of the receiving team.
Penalty: 15 yards from previous spot or awarded fair catch at spot of interference.

Section 5. Fair Catch

ARTICLE 1. When a player makes a fair catch, the ball becomes dead where caught and belongs to the receiving team at that spot.

ARTICLE 2. No player of a team or a teammate who has signalled for a fair catch may carry the ball more than two steps in any direction. *Penalty: 5 yards.*

ARTICLE 3. After a legal fair catch the receiving team may choose to snap or free kick anywhere between the inbounds line on the yard-line through the spot of the catch or through the spot of interference, if awarded.

ARTICLE 4. A valid catch signal is the extending of one arm at full arm's length above the head and waving the hand from side to side of the body more than once.

ARTICLE 5. A muffed fair catch shall be declared dead when the ball makes contact with the ground.

RULE 7—THE SCRIMMAGE, SNAPPING, HANDING, AND PASSING THE BALL

Section 1. The Scrimmage

The Start

ARTICLE 1. All players from scrimmage must be started by a legal snap from a point between the inbounds lines, unless the rules provide for a free kick.

Scrimmage

ARTICLE 2. Any infraction of the following is a foul:

a. Before the ball is snapped:

1. The Snapper, after assuming the position for the snap and adjusting the ball, may neither move nor change the position of the ball in a manner simulating the beginning of a play until it is snapped. An infraction of this provision may be penalized whether or not the ball is snapped and the penalty for any resultant encroachment or contact foul by an opponent shall be cancelled.

2. All offensive players must be within fifteen yards of the ball when it is declared ready-for-play.

3. After the ball is ready-for-play and until it is snapped, no player on defense may touch the ball, nor may any player contact opponents or in any other way interfere with them. This includes standing in the zone to give defensive signals, or shifting through the zone.

4. No player of the offensive team shall make a false start. A false start includes feigning a charge, or a play. An infraction of this rule may be penalized whether or not the ball is snapped and the penalty for any resultant encroachment or contact foul by the opponent shall be cancelled.

5. In a snap preceded by a huddle or shift, all players of the offense must come to a complete stop and remain stationary in legal position without movement of feet, body, head, or arms, for at least one full second before the ball is snapped.

6. All players, except the Snapper, must assume a position with neither hand nor knees touching the ground. (No 3 or 4 point stance.)

b. When the ball is snapped:

1. At least three players on the offensive line with 7 players, four with eight players, five with nine players, and seven with eleven players must be on their scrimmage line. The remaining players must be either on their scrimmage line or behind their backfield line, except as follows:

   One player may be between the scrimmage line and the backfield line if placed in a position to receive a hand-to-hand snap from between the Snapper's legs. When in such position, that player may receive the snap himself or it may go directly to any back.

2. All players must be inbounds and only the Snapper may be encroaching on the neutral zone, but no part of their persons may be beyond the neutral zone and their feet must be stationary behind the ball.

3. One offensive player may be in motion, but not in motion toward the opponent's goal line. If such player starts from the scrimmage line player must be at least five yards behind that line when the ball is snapped. Other offensive players must be stationary in their positions without movement of the feet, body, head or arms.

4. No offensive player, while on the scrimmage line, may receive a snap. *Penalty: Five yards and ball remains dead.*

Section 2. Handing the Ball

Handing Forward

ARTICLE 1. No player may hand the ball forward except as follows: A Team A player who is behind the scrimmage line may hand the ball forward to a backfield teammate who is also behind that line; or to a teammate who was on the scrimmage line when the ball was snapped, provided that teammate left the line position, faced his or her own end line and was at least one yard behind the scrimmage line when player received the ball.

Penalty: 5 yards from spot of foul; also, loss of down if by Team A before team possession changes during a scrimmage down.

Handing Backward

ARTICLE 2. A ball carrier may hand the ball backward at anytime.

Section 3. Backward Pass and Fumble

At Anytime

ARTICLE 1. A Ball Carrier may pass the ball backward or lose player possession by a fumble at anytime except if intentionally thrown out-of-bounds to conserve time.

Caught or Intercepted

ARTICLE 2. A backward pass or fumble may be caught in flight in-bounds by any player and advanced.

Out-of-Bounds

ARTICLE 3. A backward pass or fumble which goes out-of-bounds between the goal lines belongs to the team last in possession at the out-of-bounds spot. If out-of-bounds behind a goal line it is a touchback or safety.

Dead When Ball Hits Ground

ARTICLE 4. A backward pass or fumble which touches the ground between the goal lines is dead at the spot where it touches the ground and belongs to the team last in possession unless lost on downs.

Section 4. Forward Pass

Legal Forward Pass

ARTICLE 1. All players are eligible to receive a forward pass. During a scrimmage down and before team possession has changed, a forward pass may be thrown provided the ball, when it leaves the passer's hand, is on A's side of the defensive team's line of scrimmage. Team A may make as many forward passes as desired from in or behind the neutral zone.

Illegal Forward Pass

ARTICLE 2. A forward pass is illegal:
a. If the passer is beyond the line of scrimmage when the ball leaves the hand.
b. If thrown after team possession has changed during the down.
c. If intentionally thrown to the ground or out-of-bounds.
Penalty: 5 yards from spot of foul; also loss of down if by Team A before change of team possession during a down.

56

Eligible Receivers

ARTICLE 3. All players of both teams are eligible to touch or catch a pass.

Eligibility Lost By Going Out-of-Bounds

ARTICLE 4. An offensive player who goes out-of-bounds during a passing down loses eligibility until the ball has been touched by an opponent.
Penalty: Loss of down at previous spot.

Completed Pass

ARTICLE 5. A forward pass is completed when caught by any player of the passing team who is inbounds and the ball continues in play. If the pass is caught inbounds simultaneously by opponents, the ball becomes dead and belongs to the passing team at spot of simultaneous catch.

Incompleted Pass

ARTICLE 6. A forward pass is incomplete when the ball touches the ground or goes out-of-bounds. It is also incomplete when a player jumps from inbounds and catches the pass but lands on or outside a boundary line. An incomplete legal forward pass belongs to the passing team at the previous spot unless lost on downs. An incomplete illegal forward pass belongs to the passing team at the spot of the pass unless lost on downs.

Contact Interference

ARTICLE 7. Contact by a player which interferes with an eligible receiver who is beyond the neutral zone during a legal forward pass is pass interference unless it occurs:
a. When two or more players are making a simultaneous and bona fide attempt to reach, catch, or bat the pass.
b. When, immediately following the snap, opposing players charge into and contact opponents within one yard beyond the neutral zone.
c. When a Team B player contacts an opponent before the pass is thrown.
d. Interference beyond the line of scrimmage is prohibited by Team A from the time the ball is snapped until the pass is touched by any player. Interference by Team B is prohibited from the time the pass is thrown until it is touched by any player. The restriction does not apply if the pass does not cross the line of scrimmage.
Penalty: For pass interference—15 yards. If by A, the down counts. If by B it is first down for A. Note: If the pass interference is intentional or unsportsmanlike, the team shall be penalized an additional 15 yards.

RULE 8—SCORING

Section 1. Value of Scores

Scoring

ARTICLE 1. The following methods shall be used in scoring a game:
    a. Touchdown . . . . 6 points
    b. Field Goal . . . . 3 points
    c. Safety . . . . 2 points
    d. Successful try for point:
        (1) By running or passing . . . . 2 points
        (2) By kicking . . . . 1 point
    e. Forfeited game 1-0
    f. Penetration (tie game) . . . . 1 point

Section 2. Touchdown

When Scored

ARTICLE 1. A touchdown shall be scored for the team to which the ball legally belongs, when a down is completed and any part of the ball is on, above or behind the opponent's goal line.

Section 3. Try for Point

Opportunity To Score 1 or 2 Points

ARTICLE 1. An opportunity to score one or two points, while time is out, shall be granted a team scoring a touchdown. There shall be one scrimmage play (two points) or a kick (one point) from any point between the inbounds line on or behind the opponent's three yard line, unless the point is changed by penalty.

When Scored

ARTICLE 2. The point shall be awarded if the try results in what would have been a touchdown, or field goal, or safety under rules governing play at other times.

Foul During Try For Point

ARTICLE 3. If an Offsetting foul occurs while the ball is ready-for-play, or during the down, the down shall be replayed. When a distance penalty is incurred by Team B during a successful try, Team A shall have the option of declining the score and repeat the try following enforcement or accepting the score with enforcement of the penalty from the spot of the next kickoff. A replay after a penalty against Team B may be from any point between the inbounds lines on the yardline where the penalty leaves the ball.

Next Play

ARTICLE 4. After a try for point the next play shall be a kickoff. The Field Captain of the team which was scored upon shall designate the kicking or receiving team.

Section 4. Field Goal

When Scored

ARTICLE 1. A field goal shall be scored for the kicking team, when a drop kick (a ball dropped to the ground and kicked as it touches or rises from the ground) or a place kick (a ball kicked from a fixed position on the ground or on a tee not more than two inches removed from the ground, either held or set in a position) in flight, other than a try for point or a kick off, passes over the cross bar and over an upright or between the uprights of the receiving team's goal before touching the ground or a member of the kicking team, and no penalty incurred during the down is inflicted.

Next Play

ARTICLE 2. The play following the scoring of a field goal shall be a kickoff. The Field Captain of the team scored upon shall designate which team shall kick off.

Section 5. Touchback—Safety

When Scored

ARTICLE 1. When the ball is out-of-bounds behind a goal line (except from an incompleted forward pass), when the ball becomes dead in possession of a player on, or behind player's own goal line, it is a touchback if the attacking team is responsible for the ball being on or behind the goal line; if the defending team is responsible, it is a safety. When an accepted penalty for a foul or an illegal forward pass leaves the ball on or behind the offending team's goal line it is a safety.

Responsibility

ARTICLE 2. The team responsible for a ball being on, above, or behind a goal line is the team whose player carries the ball to or across that goal line or imparts to the ball an impetus which forces it to or across that line; or incurs a penalty which leaves the ball on or behind that line.

Initial Impetus

ARTICLE 3. The impetus imparted by a player who kicks, passes, snaps or fumbles the ball shall be considered responsible for the ball's progress in any direction even though its course be deflected, or reversed, after striking the ground or after striking a player of either team. However, the initial impetus is considered expended and a new impetus is provided if a loose ball is illegally kicked or batted or it is contacted again after coming to rest.

Resulting From Foul

ARTICLE 4. When the penalty for a foul committed when the ball is loose leaves the ball behind the offender's goal line it is a safety; if behind the offended team's goal line, it is a touchback.

Play After Safety

ARTICLE 5. After a safety is scored, the ball shall belong to the defending team at its own 20 yard line and that team shall put the ball in play by a free kick which may be a punt, drop kick or place kick.

Play After Touchback

ARTICLE 6. After a touchback is declared, the ball shall belong to the defending team at its own 20-yard line and that team shall put the ball in play by a snap.

Section 6. Tie Game

Overtime Period

ARTICLE 1. When the game ends in a tie score, the ball shall be placed in the center of the field, and the Referee shall toss a coin in the presence of the two Field Captains. The Captain winning the toss shall have the option of putting the ball in play by scrimmage in the first or last play of the eight alternating plays, four plays for each team, or the choice of direction of play. The loser has the remaining choice.

Additional Overtimes

ARTICLE 2. In case any overtime period ends leaving the ball at the mid-field spot, or in line with the mid-field spot where the play originally began, and the score is still tied, an additional overtime period of four alternating plays, two plays for each team, shall be played under the same conditions as the first overtime period.

Alternating Plays

ARTICLE 3. The team elected to start the series shall put the ball in play by scrimmage. At the completion of that play, their opponents shall become the offensive team, and put the ball in play at the spot where the previous play left it. Any gain or loss of distance shall be considered as a part of the play unless affected by penalty. This alternating of plays shall continue until each team has had four plays in the series of eight or two plays in a series of four.

Penalties During Overtime

ARTICLE 4. Penalties shall be interpreted according to the regular rules of touch and flag football. *Exception: Loss of down part of penalities does not apply.*

Running and Passing Plays

ARTICLE 5. Each play shall begin by scrimmage, and shall be limited to running and passing plays. No kicks from scrimmage are permitted except a kick of a try for point following a touchdown.

Intercepted Legal Forward Pass

ARTICLE 6. If a player of the defensive team intercepts a legal forward pass, the ball remains alive and the intercepting player may return it. When touched, **or when his flag is removed,** it is dead at that spot.

Winning Team

ARTICLE 7. The team penetrating, or advancing the ball into their opponent's territory, after the completion of a series of eight alternating plays, shall be declared the winner, unless other scores have been made by either team during the overtime period. In case a touchdown is scored, play shall resume after the try for point by a scrimmage at the center of the field and the series shall be completed, unless that play was the last of the series.

RULE 9—CONDUCT OF PLAYERS AND OTHERS SUBJECT TO THE RULES

Section 1. Deliberate or Flagrant Fouls

Suspension From The Game

ARTICLE 1. Whenever, in the judgement of any game official, the following acts are deliberate or flagrant, the players involved shall be suspended from the game:
a. Using fists, kicking or kneeing.
b. Using locked hands, elbows or any part of the forearm or hand, except according to rule.
c. Tackling the ball carrier as in regulation football.
d. Roughing the kicker or holder of a kick.
e. Any other deliberate or flagrant act.

Prohibited Acts

ARTICLE 2. There shall be no unsportsmanlike conduct by players, substitutes, coaches or others subject to the rules.
a. Using any act of unsportsmanlike conduct including:
(1) Abusive or insulting language.

(2) Any act of unfair play.

(3) Managers, coaches or others on the field of play at any time without permission, or their interference of any nature with the progress of the game.

(4) Players leaving the field of play other than during the intermission at half time.

(5) A substitute or any other person interfering with a player or any play while the ball is alive.

(6) Using a "hide out play" by placing a player or players near the side line who were not within 15 yards of the ball at the ready-for-play signal.

(7) The punter delaying the kick, after requesting protection.

(8) Attempting to substitute a suspended player.

(9) **Pulling or removing a flag from an offensive player without the ball by a defensive player intentionally or inadvertently.**

Penalty: 15 yards, and if flagrant, offender shall be disqualified.

Section 2. Unfair Acts

Unfair Acts

ARTICLE 1. If a team refuses to play within the two minutes after ordered to play by the Referee, or if play is interfered with by an obviously unfair or unsportsmanlike act not specifically covered by the rules; or if a team repeatedly commits fouls which can be penalized only by halving the distance to its goal line, the Refereee may enforce any penalty he considers equitable, including the awarding of a score. For, refusal to play, or for repeated fouls, the Referee shall, after one warning, forfeit the game to the opponents.

Section 3.. Personal Fouls

Player Restrictions

ARTICLE 1. No player shall commit a personal foul during a period or during an intermission. Any act prohibited hereunder or any other act of unnecessary roughness is a personal foul.

a. No player shall block in a manner that would cause his or her feet, knees or legs to strike an opponent. All blocking shall be done with the feet in contact with the ground.

b. There shall be no high-low blocking.

c. There shall be no two-on-one blocking except as indicated by rule.

d. There shall be no tripping; there shall be no clipping.

e. There shall be no contact with an opponent who is on the ground.

f. The runner shall not be thrown to the ground.

g. There shall be no hurdling. Hurdling shall be interpreted as an attempt by the runner to jump over a player with both feet or knees of the runner foremost.

h. No player shall contact an opponent obviously out of the play either before or after the ball is declared dead.

i. There shall be no unnecessary roughness of any nature.

j. **The Ball Carrier shall not deliberately drive or run into a defensive player.**

Penalty: 15 yards — Flagrant offenders may be disqualified.

Section 4. Use of Hands and Arms When Ball is in Possession

Helping the Runner

ARTICLE 1. The Ball Carrier shall not grasp a teammate or be grasped, pulled or pushed by a teammate.
Penalty: 5 yards.

Offensive Use of Hands

ARTICLE 2. **The offensive team shall be prohibited from obstructing an opponent with extended hand or arm. This includes the use of a "stiffarm" extended to ward of an opponent attempting to deflag.**
Penalty: 15 yards.

Blocking And Interlocked Interference

ARTICLE 3. Players of either team may block opponents provided it is neither forward pass interference, interference with opportunity to catch a kick, nor a personal foul. Teammates of a Ball Carrier or Passer may interfere by blocking, but there shall be no interlocking interference. This prohibition includes grasping or encircling one another, to any degree, with the hand or arm.
Penalty: 15 yards.

Leaving Feet to Obtain Possession of Ball

ARTICLE 4. No player may leave the ground with both feet in an attempt to gain possession of a ball which is rolling on the ground.
Penalty: 15 yards.

Protecting Flags

ARTICLE 5. **Ball Carriers shall not protect their Flags by blocking with arms or hands the opportunity of an opponent to pull or remove a Flag.**
Penalty: 15 yards.

Obstruction of Ball Carrier

ARTICLE 6. **The defensive player shall not hold, grasp, or obstruct forward progress of a Ball Carrier when in the act of removing a Flag.**
Penalty: 15 yards.

Blocking

ARTICLE 7. Players shall be limited to the following: 1) In all instances blockers must be on their feet when blocking. Accidentally falling when attempting a block is not an illegal block. 2) When using a hand or forearm to block, the elbow must be entirely outside the shoulder. 3) The blocker's hands may not be locked. 4) The blocker may not swing, throw, or flip the elbow or forearm. 5) The hands may be closed or cupped but the palms may not be facing the opponent being blocked. 6) There shall be no two on one blocking beyond the line of scrimmage. 7) Blocking below the waist is illegal. *Penalty: Illegal block. 15 yards.*

Use of Hands

ARTICLE 8. Players may use their hands to grasp, push or pull an opponent in an attempt to get at the Ball Carrier, and may also use their hands for protection in warding off an opponent, or to get at a loose ball.

Section 5. Batting and Kicking

Batting a Free Ball

ARTICLE 1. While a pass is in *flight,* any player may bat the ball in any direction. No player shall bat any other loose ball in flight forward in the field of play, or in any direction if it is in an end zone.
Penalty: 15 yards.

Illegally Kicking Ball

ARTICLE 2. No player shall deliberately kick a loose ball, a pass, or a ball being held for a place kick by an opponent.
Penalty: 15 yards.

RULE 10—ENFORCEMENT OF PENALTIES

Section 1. Procedure After a Foul

ARTICLE 1. *When a foul occurs during a live ball,* the referee shall, at the end of the down, notify the offended captain of his options. If the penalty is declined or there is a double foul, there is no loss of distance. A captain's choice of options may not be revoked.

ARTICLE 2. *When a foul occurs during a dead ball between downs or prior to a free kick or a snap,* the ball does not become alive. The referee shall notify the offended captain of his options.

ARTICLE 3. *When a live ball is followed by a dead ball foul by the opponent,* the penalties are administered separately and in the order of occurrence.

Section 2. Double and Multiple Fouls

ARTICLE 1. When both teams commit live ball fouls during the same live ball period and (a) there is no change of team possession, or (b) there was a change of team possession and the team in possession at the end of the down had fouled prior to final change of possession, it is a double foul. In (a) or (b) the penalties cancel and the down is replayed.

ARTICLE 2. If both teams foul during a down where there is a change of team possession, the team last gaining possession may retain the ball, provided it did not foul prior to the final change of possession and it declined the penalty for its opponent's foul.

ARTICLE 3. When two or more live ball fouls are committed by the same team, only one penalty may be chosen except when a foul(s) for unsportsmanlike conduct follows a previous foul. In such a case, the penalty(s) for the unsportsmanlike conduct is administered separately. The offended captain may choose which penalty will be administered or he may decline all penalties.

ARTICLE 4. Penalties for dead balls fouls are administered separately and in the order of occurrence. Dead ball fouls are not coupled with live ball fouls or other dead ball fouls to create double or multiple fouls. Penalize all unsportsmanlike fouls separately, *and in addition to those occuring during a down by the same team.*

Section 3. Types of Play and Basic Enforcement Spots

ARTICLE 1. If a foul occurs during a down, the basic enforcement spot is fixed by the type of play. There are two types of play: (a) a loose ball play, and (b) a running play.

a. A loose ball play is action during
1. a free kick.
2. a scrimmage kick.
3. a legal forward pass.
4. a backward pass or a fumble by A from on or behind the scrimmage line.
5. a loose ball play also includes the run which precedes a legal pass, kick, or fumble.

NOTE: When a foul occurs during a loose ball play, the basic enforcement spot is the previous spot. However, if the foul is by the offense and occurs behind the basic enforcement spot, it is from the spot of the foul.

NOTE: When a foul occurs during a running play, the basic enforcement spot is where the related run ends, which is where the ball becomes dead or where the player loses possession. However, if the foul is by the offense and occurs behind the basic enforcement spot, it is from the spot of the foul.

Section 4. Administering Penalties

ARTICLE 1. The penalty for a foul between downs is enforced from the succeeding spot.

ARTICLE 2. The penalty for a foul which occurs simultaneously with a snap or free kick is enforced from the previous spot, which is the spot of the snap or free kick.

Section 5. Special Enforcements

ARTICLE 1. A measurement cannot take the ball more than half the distance from the enforcement spot to the offending team's goal line. If the penalty is greater than this, the ball is placed halfway from the enforcement spot to the goal line.

ARTICLE 2. If the offensive team throws an illegal forward pass from its end zone or commits any other foul on or behind its goal line for which the penalty is accepted, it is a safety. For a defensive team foul on or behind the offended team's goal measurement, it is from the goal line.

ARTICLE 3. A disqualified player must always leave the game.

ARTICLE 4. A referee's decision to forfeit a game must be accepted by both teams.

NOTE: There are some tenets or basic rules which are established for flag football because of legal or illegal removal of flags which do not apply to regular or touch football. These follow:

(1) Deflagging (one or more flags) is only allowed under special circumstances similiar to tackling in football. Offensive players must have possession of the ball before they can legally be deflagged.

(2) A flag(s) removed inadvertently (not removed by grabbing and pulling) does not cause play to stop. It should continue as if the flag(s) had not been removed.

(3) In circumstances where a flag(s) is removed inadvertently or illegally (accidentally) the play should continue with the option of the penalty or the play.

(4) In all situations where a play is in progress and a ball carrier loses one or all flags (rare) either accidentally, inadvertently, or on purpose, the deflagging reverts to a one-hand touch of the ball carrier between the waist and the knees.

CHAPTER VI

Illustrated Touch and Flag Football Rules

The illustrated rules which are presented in this chapter have been selected in an attempt to help officials develop a visual, mental image of game situations. Hopefully, these images will assist individuals in recognizing, understanding, and reacting properly to events as they occur on the field.

Rule: 2 Section 18: Article 1. When the flag is clearly taken from a ball carrier, the down shall end and the ball is declared dead.

Rule: 2 Section 24: Article 1. Touching is the placing of one or both hands anywhere between the shoulders and knees of an opponent with the ball.

Rule 2: Section 27: Article 1. Deflagging is the legal removal of a flag of an opponent in possession of the ball.

Rule 3: Section 3: Article 4. Each team is entitled to three time-outs during each half without penalty.

Rule 3: Section 3: Article 6. A free time-out requested by the Field Captain shall not exceed 1½ minutes. Any time-out, however, may be extended by the Referee for the benefit of a seriously injured player.

Rule 4: Section 1: Article 3b. A live ball becomes dead when any part of the Ball Carrier's person other than a hand or foot touches the ground.

Rule 4: Section 1: Article 3g. A live ball becomes dead when a backward pass or fumble by a player touches the ground.

Rule 4: Section 1: Article 3m. A live ball becomes dead when an official sounds the whistle (even if inadvertently).

Rule 5: Section 1: Article 3. The line to gain in any series shall be the zone in advance of the ball, unless distance has been lost due to penalty or failure to gain.

Rule 5: Section 2: Article 8. If offsetting fouls occur during a down, or while the ball is ready-for-play for such down, that down shall be repeated.

Rule 6: Section 1: Article 1. A free kick begins each half of a game, and begins play following a touchdown, field goal, or safety.

Rule 6: Section 1: Article 3. For any free kick information, the kicking team's restraining line shall be the yard-line through the forward-most point from which the ball may be kicked.

Rule 6: Section 1: Article 4. A free kick touched by a player of the receiving team, which then touches the ground, is dead at the spot at which it touches the ground and belongs to the receiving team.

Rule 6: Section 3: Article 2. When a scrimmage kick is to be made, the kicking team must announce it to the referee before the ball is declared ready-for-play.

Rule 6: Section 3: Article 4. The kicker must be at least 5 yards behind the line of scrimmage when receiving the snap.

Rule 6: Section 3: Article 6. No player of the kicking team shall touch a scrimmage kick which goes beyond the neutral zone before it touches an opponent.

Rule 6: Section 3: Article 5. Except on a try-for-point, a scrimmage kick which fails to cross the scrimmage line continues in play and all players are eligible to catch or recover the ball and advance it.

Rule 6: Section 3: Article 9. A player who is pushed or blocked into a scrimmage kick which has crossed the neutral zone shall not be considered as having touched the unless the player's hand touched it.

Rule 6: Section 3: Article 11. If a player of the kicking team who is beyond the neutral zone catches or recovers a scrimmage kick, the ball becomes dead and belongs to the kicking team.

Rule 6: Section 4: Article 1. A player of the receiving team who is so located that he/she could catch a scrimmage kick which is beyond the neutral zone and in flight, must be given an unencumbered opportunity to catch the ball.

Rule 6: Section 5: Article 1. When a player makes a fair catch, the ball becomes dead where caught and belongs to the receiving team at that spot.

Rule 6: Section 5: Article 4. A valid fair catch signal is the extending of one arm at full arm's length above the head and waving the hand from side to side of the body more than once.

Rule 7: Section 2: Article 2b-3. When the ball is snapped, one offensive player may be in motion, but not in motion toward the opponent's goal line.

Rule 7: Section 3: Article 2. A backward pass or fumble may be caught in flight inbounds by any player and advanced.

Rule 7: Section 3: Article 4. A backward pass or fumble which touches the ground between the goals is dead at the spot where it touches the ground and belongs to the team last in possession unless lost on downs.

Rule 7: Section 4: Article 1. All players are eligible to receive a forward pass.

Rule 7: Section 4: Article 2a. A forward pass is illegal if the passer is beyond the line of scrimmage when the ball leaves the hand.

Rule 7: Section 4: Article 4. An offensive player who goes out-of-bounds during a passing down loses eligibility until the ball has been touched by an opponent.

Rule 7: Section 4: Article 6. A forward pass is incomplete when the ball touches the ground or goes out-of-bounds.

Rule 7: Section 4: Article 7. Contact by a player which interfers with an eligible receiver who is beyond the neutral zone during a legal forward pass is pass interference.

Rule 7: Section 4: Article 7d. Interference beyond the line of scrimmage is prohibited by Team A *from the time the ball is snapped until* the pass is touched by any player. Interference by Team B is prohibited from the time the pass is thrown *until* it is touched by any player.

Rule 8: Section 5: Article 1. A safety is scored when the ball becomes dead in possession of a player behind, on, or above the player's goal line.

Rule 9: Section 1: Article 1e. Whenever, in the judgement of any game official, a player commits a deliberate or flagrant foul, the player involved shall be suspended from the game.

Rule 9: Section 1: Article 2a-6. It is unsportsmanlike conduct to use a "hide out play" by placing a player or players near the side line who were not within 15 yards of the ball at the ready-for-play signal.

Rule 9: Section 2: Article 1. If play is interfered with by an obviously unfair or unsportsmanlike act not specifically covered by the rules, the Referee may enforce any penalty he/she considers equitable, including the awarding of a score.

Rule 9: Section 5: Article 1a. No player shall block in a manuever that would cause his/her feet, knees, or legs to strike an opponent. All blocking shall be done with the feet in contact with the ground.

Rule 9: Section 3: Article 1c. There shall be no two-on-one blocking except as permissible by rule.

Rule 9: Section 3: Article 1f. The runner shall not be thrown to the ground.

Rule 9: Section 3: Article 1i. There shall be no unnecessary roughness of *any* nature.

Rule 9: Section 3: Article 1j. The ball carrier shall not deliberately drive or run into a defensive player.

Rule 9: Section 4: Article 1. The ball carrier shall not grasp a teammate or be grasped, pulled or pushed by a teammate.

Rule 9: Section 4: Article 2. "Stiffarming" or obstructing an opponent with an extended hand or arm in an attempt to ward off being deflagged is prohibited.

Rule 9: Section 4: Article 5. Ball carriers shall not protect their flags by blocking with arms or hands the opportunity of an opponent to pull or remove a flag.

Rule 9: Section 4: Article 6. The defensive player shall not hold, grasp, or obstruct the forward progress of a ball carrier when in the act of removing a flag.

CHAPTER VII

Officials' Signals and Penalties

Football officials utilize a series of signs and signals to inform and make their decisions known to players, coaches and spectators during a game. An official is ready to officiate a contest when he/she knows and understands when and how to use signals properly. A properly executed signal adds to the pleasure and enjoyment of the game by informing spectators what has transpired or what is taking place. It also helps officials win the respect of players, coaches and spectators alike by demonstrating to them their professionalism in administering the rules.

The following illustrations represent the Official Touch and Flag Football "language" used by officials throughout the United States. While in some instances an official may develop mannerisms that constitute a slight variation from the "officials signals". These variations should not modify or change the prescribed signals in such a manner to the point of disguising them. Some degree of individuality, however, in the interpretation and execution of these signals is usually acceptable.

It is not sufficient merely for an official to know how to perform the signals. An official should also learn how to time and deliver the signals so everyone involved can clearly receive the message being presented. The proper sense of timing and delivery can best be learned through practice and experience.

Before giving a signal, the official should pause momentarily. This pause enables everyone to focus their attention on the official. Then in a clear and precise manner, the official should perform the signal to inform everyone of the infraction that occured and the ensuing decision by the offended team. This signal should be given both prior to and after the decision has been made and the penalty administered.

In summary, an official should execute the prescribed signals clearly, correctly and precisely. An official should not show off. He/she should remember that clear signals are an integral part of the game.

1. Encroachment or violation of free-kick rules.

2. False start. Illegal position or procedure. Illegal forward handing.

3. Illegal Motion

4. Illegal Shift

5. Start the clock.

6. Delay of game. Crawling.

7. Personal Foul

8. Clipping

9. Roughing the Kicker

10. Unsportsmanlike conduct. Delay start of half. Illegal participation.

11. Illegal use of Hands and Arms

12. Intentional Grounding

13. Illegally Passing or Handing Ball Forward

14. Interference with fair catch or forward pass.

15. Illegally kicking or batting a loose ball. First touching of a kick.

16. Incomplete Forward Pass, Penalty Declined, No Play, or No Score

17. Pushing, helping runner or interlocked interference.

18. Dead ball foul (Follow with foul signal). If waved side to side: Touch back.

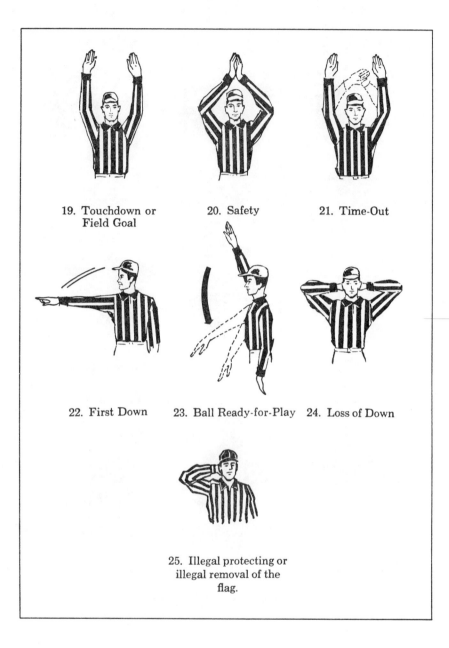

19. Touchdown or Field Goal

20. Safety

21. Time-Out

22. First Down

23. Ball Ready-for-Play

24. Loss of Down

25. Illegal protecting or illegal removal of the flag.

Touch and Flag Football Official's Signals

1. **Offside, Encroachment or Violation of Free-Kick Rules.** Place the hands on the hips. PENALTY: 5 yards
2. **False Start, Illegal Position or Procedure and Illegal Forward Handing.** Rotate the forearms over and over in front of the chest. PENALTY: 5 yards.
3. **Illegal Motion.** Make a horizontal arc with either hand in front of the chest. PENALTY: 5 yards.
4. **Illegal Shift.** Raise both arms in front of the chest with the finger tips touching, the palms facing down and the forearms horizontal to the ground. PENALTY: 5 yards.
5. **Start the Clock.** Swing the arm in full circle to simulate a winding clock.
6. **Encroachment, Delay of Game or Crawling.** Fold the arms in front of the body. PENALTY: 5 yards.
7. **Personal Foul.** Raise both arms in front of the body and strike at one wrist.
8. **Clipping.** Strike at the back of the calf with one hand. PENALTY: 15 yards.
9. **Roughing the Kicker.** Swing one leg forward in a kicking motion. PENALTY: 15 yards.
10. **Unsportsmanlike Conduct, Delay Start of Half or Illegal Participation.** Arms outstretched to each side with the palms facing down. PENALTY: 15 yards.
11. **Illegal use of Hands and Arms.** Grasp the wrist of one hand at chest level. PENALTY: 15 yards
12. **Intentional Grounding.** Raise both arms to one side keeping them parallel to each other and swing them simultaneously in a downward motion. PENALTY: 5 yards and Loss of Down.
13. **Illegal Passing or Handling Ball Forward.** Place and wave one hand behind the back. PENALTY: 5 yards and Loss of Down.
14. **Interference with Forward Pass or Fair Catch.** Raise hands to shoulder level and move them forward in a pushing motion with the hands remaining vertical to the ground. PENALTY: 15 yards.
15. **Illegally Kicking or Batting a Loose Ball or First Touching of a Kick.** PENALTY: 15 yards.
16. **Incomplete Forward Pass, Penalty Declined, No Play or No Score.** Move the hands back and forth in a crossing movement in front of the body.
17. **Pushing, Helping Runner or Interlocked Interference.** Indicate a pushing movement with the arms down and the hands to the front. PENALTY: 15 yards.
18. **Dead Ball Foul (Follow with foul signal). If waved to the side: Touchback.** Extend one arm, hand open above the head for a dead ball foul. Wave the arm to the side for a touchback.
19. **Touchdown or Field Goal.** Extend both arms with the hands open above the head.
20. **Safety.** Raise both arms above the head with the palms touching.
21. **Time-out.** Raise and criss-cross the hands above the head.
22. **First Down.** Raise and extend the arm at shoulder level and point it toward the defensive team's goal.
23. **Ball Ready-For-Play.** Raise and extend an arm open hand above the head and then lower it to the side.
24. **Loss of Down.** Place the palms of both hands behind and touching the back of the head with the elbows pointing to the side.
25. **Illegal Protecting or Illegal Removal of the Flag.** Place the palm of one hand behind and touching the back of the head with the elbow pointing to the side. PENALTY: 15 yards.

SUMMARY OF PENALTIES

O, OFFICIALS' SIGNALS (SEE PAGES 78, 79, 80), WITH THE NUMBERS REFERRING TO THE NUMBERED ILLUSTRATIONS; R, RULES; S, SECTION; A, ARTICLE

Loss of a Down

	O	R	S	A
Illegally handling ball forward (also loss of 5 yards)	13	7	2	1
Illegal forward pass by Team A (also loss of 5 yards)	13	7	4	2
Intentionally grounding pass (also loss of 5 yards)	12	7	4	2
Offensive pass interference (also loss of 15 yards)	14	7	4	7

Loss of 5 Yards

	O	R	S	A
Excess time-out illegally used or requested	6	3	3	5
Illegal delay of the game	6	3	4	2
Putting ball in play before declared ready-for-play	2	3	4	2
Infraction of free kick formation	1	6	1	2
Illegal snap	2	7	1	2
Infraction of scrimmage formation	1	7	1	2
Interference with opponents or the ball	2	7	1	2
Offensive player illegally in motion at the snap	3	7	1	2
False start or simulating start of a play	2	7	1	2
Player on line receiving snap	2	7	1	2
Illegally handing ball forward (also loss of down if by Team A)	13	7	2	1
Intentionally grounding pass (also loss of a down)	12	7	4	2
Illegal kick	15	6	3	1
Illegal shift	4	7	1	2
Interlocked Interference	7	9	4	3
Helping the Runner	17	9	4	1

Loss of 15 Yards

	O	R	S	A
Team not ready to play at start of either half	6	3	4	1
Interference with opportunity to catch a kick	14	6	4	1
Forward pass interference (also the down counts if by A and a new series if by B)	14	7	4	7
Striking, kicking, kneeing, elbowing, etc.	10	9	1	1
Meeting with knee, striking with open hand, etc.	7	9	1	1
Roughing the kicker or holder	9	9	1	1
Unsportsmanlike conduct	10	9	1	2
Persons illegally on the field	10	9	1	2
Hurdling	7	9	3	1
Tripping	7	9	3	1
Running into opponent	7	9	1	2
Clipping	8	9	3	1
Illegal use of hand or arm by offense	11	9	4	2
Protecting flags	7	9	4	5
Illegal removal of flag	10	9	1	2
Obstructing ball carrier	7	9	4	6

Violation

	O	R	S	A
Illegal touching of free kick by kicking team (offended team's ball at spot)	15	6	1	4
Illegal touching of scrimmage kick	15	6	3	5
Loss of half distance to goal line if distance penalty exceeds half the distance	10	5	1	

GLOSSARY OF TERMS

BALL CARRIER
The player who runs with the ball. R-2, S-23, A-6.

BLOCK
To legally obstruct an opponent by contacting them with any part of the blocker.
body. R-2, S-4, A-7.

BLOCKER
An offensive player who legally makes a block. R-2, S-2, A-1.

BLOCKING
See BLOCK.

CAPTAIN
A member of the team who is appointed or elected to represent the team as its
spokesperson. R-1, S-1, A-5.

CLIPPING
To block an opponent from behind by throwing or dropping the body across the back
of an opponents legs. R-2, S-3, A-3.

COACH
The indiviudal who instructs and trains the players in the various fundamentals and
techniques of the game. This individual is also in charge of the strategy employed in
the game.

COIN TOSS
The flip of the coin that takes place prior to the game to determine who kicks, who
receives and what goal each team defends.

DEAD BALL
A ball that is not in play. R-2, S-1, A-1, R-4, S-1, A-1.

DEAD BALL SPOT
The point at which the ball last became dead. R-2, S-22, A-4

DEFENSE
To prevent a team from advancing the ball or from scoring.

DEFENSIVE TEAM
The team not in possession of the ball. R-2, S-23, A-1.

DEFLAGGING
The legal removal of a flag of an opponent in possession of the ball. R-2, S-27, A-1.

DELAY OF GAME
Failing to legally put the ball in play within a specified time. R-3, S-4, A-1and 2.

DOWN
A unit of the game which starts after the ball is ready-for-play with a snap or free kick
and ends when the ball next becomes dead. R-2, S-4, a-1.

DOWNFIELD
The part of the field toward which the offensive team is headed.

DOWN MARKER
The piece of equipment used to indicate the number of the down. R-1, S-1, A-6.

ENCROACHMENT
When a player is illegally in the neutral zone.

ENFORCEMENT SPOT
The spot or point from which the penalty for a foul is enforced. R-2, S-22, A-1.

FAIR CATCH
To catch a kicked ball beyond the neutral zone after signaling to the officials that the ball will not be advanced. The player must signal by raising and waving one arm and hand above his head. R-6, S-5, A-1 thru 5.

FIELD
The playing area for a touch or flag football game. R-1, S-2, A-1.

FIELD GOAL
A ball kicked from scrimmage either by dropkicking or placekicking it through the goalposts and over the crossbar of the opposing team. R-8, S-4, A-1

FIELD JUDGE
A football official who assumes a position in the defensive backfield and who is primarily responsible for deep pass plays and punts.

FIRST DOWN
The first of a series of four downs in which a team must get to the next zone line to gain in order to retain possession of the ball.

FLAGRANT FOUL
An act or foul that is committed by a player and is considered deliberate in the judgment of any game official. R-9, S-1, A-4.

FLAGS
The piece of equipment attached to a belt on each side of the body and worn by every player. R-1, S-1, A-1.

FORWARD PASS
A ball that is thrown in a direction forward of the passer. R-7, S-4, A-1.

FOUL
An infraction of the playing rules. R-2, S-6, A-1

FOURTH DOWN
The last down in a series of downs before change of ball possession takes place unless another first down is awarded.

FREE BALL
A live ball not in player-possession. R-2, S-1, A-2

FREE KICK
An unhindered kick. R-2, S-12, A-5

FUMBLE
The accidental loss of control or possession of the ball. R-2, S-7, A-1.

GOAL LINE
A vertical plane extending the width of the field separating an end zone from the playing field. R-1, S-1, A-2, and R-2, S-8, A-1.

HALF TIME
The time between each half of the game.

HANDING-THE-BALL
The act of transferring the ball from one teammate to another without throwing, fumbling or kicking it. R-2, S-9, A-1.

HOLDING
To impede the progress of an opposing player by grasping that player with the hands or arms.

Glossary of Terms

HUDDLE
Two or more offensive players grouped together after the ball is ready-for-play to receive assignments before assuming a scrimmage formation of the snap of the ball. R-2, S-10, A-1.

HURDLING
To jump over a player while running. R-2, S-11, A-1.

ILLEGAL MOTION
When an offensive player is moving forward or more than one offensive player is moving backward or laterally at the snap.

ILLEGAL-USE-OF-HANDS
To use the hands in a manner not in accordance with the rules.

INCOMPLETED PASS
A pass that s not caught or itercepted. R-7, S-4, A-6.

INTENTIONAL GROUNDING
The act of deliberately throwing the ball to the ground.

KICK
The act of propelling the ball by striking it with the foot. R-2, S-12, A-1 thru 7.

KICKER
The player who kicks or is designated to kick the ball. R-2, S-23, A-2.

KICKOFF
A place kick which starts each half and follows each try-for-point, safety or field goal. R-2, S-12, A-6.

LATERAL
A pass that is thrown in any direction other than towards the opponents goal line.

LINEMAN
Any player on either the offensive or defensive team who play on the line-of-scrimmage.

LINE-OF-SCRIMMAGE
See SCRIMMAGE LINE.

LINESMAN
A football official who assumes a position at the sideline on the line-of-scrimmage and is primarily responsible for watching for offsides, encroachment and that the passer does not cross the line-of-scrimmage before passing the ball.

LINE-TO-GAIN
See ZONE-LINE-TO-GAIN.

LIVE BALL
A ball that is in play. R-2, S-1, A-1.

MEASUREMENT OF DISTANCE
To establish the distance gained or lost in a down. R-5, S-1, A-1.

MECHANICS
The procedure the officials utilize to observe play, enforce and administer rules and keep the game running smoothly.

NEUTRAL ZONES
An imaginary area the width of the football. It is the space between the two lines of scrimmage and is established when the ball is ready-for-play. R-2, S-14, A-1.

Glossary of Terms

OFFENSE
To try to advance the ball to score.

OFFENSIVE TEAM
The team in possession of the ball. R-2, S-23, A-1.

OFFICIAL
One of the individuals (referee, linesman, umpire or field judge) who administer the rules of the game.

OFFICIAL BALL
The ball that is designated for play and meets the recommendations for size and shape for regulation football. R-1, S-3, A-1 and 2

OFFICIALS' SIGNALS
The body signs and signals utilized by officials to indicate what is taking place during the game.

OFFSIDES
The position of a player except the snapper or the kicker and holder of a place kick, whose person or any part is beyond his scrimmage line when the ball is put into play. R-2, S-15, A-1.

OUT-OF-BOUNDS
On or over the sideline or touching anyone or anything that is out-of-bounds other than an official. R-4, S-2, A-1 thru 4.

PASS
See FORWARD PASS.

PASSER
The player who has thrown a legal forward pass. R-2, S-23, A-4.

PASS INTERFERENCE
Hampering a player who is about to catch a forward pass. R-7, S-4, A-7.

PENALTY
A loss imposed by rule upon a team which has committed a foul. R-2, S-17, A-1.

PENETRATION
Advancement of the ball into the opponents territory. R-8, S-6, A-7

PERIOD
A time division of the game. Synonymous with QUARTER.

PREVIOUS SPOT
The point from which the ball was last put in play. R-2, S-22, A-2.

PUNT
The act of kicking the ball by a player who drops it and kicks it before it strikes the ground. R-2, S-12, A-2.

QUARTER
Any of the four divisions of the football game. Also see PERIOD.

READY-FOR-PLAY
The time period declared by the officials when the ball can be put in play. R-4, S-1, A-4.

REFEREE
The principal official on the field who assumes a position in the offensive backfield.

Glossary of Terms

RULES
The laws of the game.

SAFETY
A score of two points awarded the defensive team when a ball carrier is caught, steps out-of-bounds or loses control of the ball in the end zone. R-8, S-5, A-1 thru 5.

SCORE
A count showing the number of points made by each team. R-8, S-1, A-1.

SCRIMMAGE KICK
A punt or field goal that is made by a team on a play that begins with a snap. R-2, S-2, A-7.

SCRIMMAGE LINE
The yard-line and its vertical plane for each team which passes through the point of the ball nearest its own goal line. R-2, S-19, A-2.

SERIES
Four consecutive downs to advance the ball to the next zone by scrimmage. R-5, S-1, A-2.

SHIFT
A simultaneous change of position by two or more offensive players after they have lined up for the snap. R-2, S-20, A-1.

SNAP
The method of putting the ball in play from scrimmage with the center handing the ball back between his legs to a back positioned behind him. R-2, S-23, A-7.

SNAPPER
The player who snaps the ball. R-2, S-23, A-7

SPOT-OF-FOUL
The point at which the foul occurs. R-2, S-22, A-5.

SUBSTITUTE
A player who replaces another player already in the game. R-2, S-23, A-8.

TACKLING
To knock the ball carrier to the ground or to stop his forward progress.

TIME OUT
A brief suspension of play declared by the official. R-3, S-3, A-1 thru 8.

TOUCH
See TOUCHING.

TOUCHBACK.
A situation in which a player downs the ball in his own end zone after it was propelled over the goal line by the opposing team via a punt, kickoff or pass. R-8, s-5, A-1 thru 6.

TOUCHDOWN
A score of six points by either team carrying the ball across the opponents goal, recovering a loose ball in the opponents end zone or by completing a forward pass to a teammate across the goal line. R-8, S-2, A-1.

TRIPPING
Using the lower leg or foot to obstruct an opponent below the knee. r-2, S-25, A-1.

TRY-FOR-POINT
An attempt awarded a team after they scored a touchdown to try to score an additional one or two points. R-8, S-3, A-1.

25-SECOND COUNT
The time interval after the ball is declared ready-for-play and put into play. R-4, S-1, A-5.

UMPIRE
An official who assumes a position in the defensive backfield and is primarily responsible for checking players equipment, watching for offensive and defensive holding and for linemen illegally downfield on passing and kicking plays.

UNSPORTSMANLIKE CONDUCT
Conduct that is not characteristic of good sportsmanship. For example, fighting, using profanity, striking an official, etc.

VIOLATION
A rule infraction for which no penalty is prescribed and which does not offset the penalty for a foul. R-2, S-6, A-1.

YARDLINE
A line in the field of play parallel to the endline between the goal lines. R-2, S-26, A-1.

ZONE-LINE-TO-GAIN
The line to gain in any series shall be the zone in advance of the ball unless distance has been lost due to penalty or failure to gain. R-5, S-1, A-3.